Why Believe in Jesus?

WHY BELIEVE IN JESUS?

Evangelistic Reflections for Lent

DONALD ENGLISH

Epworth Press

© Donald English 1986

All rights reserved. No part of this publication
may be reproduced, stored in a retrieval system,
or transmitted, in any form or by any means,
electronic, mechanical, photocopying, recording
or otherwise, without the prior permission of the
publisher, Epworth Press.

British Library Cataloguing in Publication Data

English, Donald
 Why believe in Jesus?: evangelistic reflections
 for Lent.
 1. Jesus Christ
 I. Title
 232   BT202

ISBN 0-7162-0417-7

First published 1986
by Epworth Press
Room 195, 1 Central Buildings,
Westminster, London SW1H 9NR

Typeset at The Spartan Press Ltd
and printed in Great Britain by
Richard Clay (The Chaucer Press) Ltd
Bungay, Suffolk

For Richard

CONTENTS

	Foreword	ix
1	How Shall We Describe Him?	1
2	What Did He Teach?	18
3	What Difference Does It Make?	32
4	Why Was He Killed?	47
5	How Could He Be Raised From Death?	60
6	How Can He Be Known?	71
	References	82

FOREWORD

Readers deserve to know the origin of this book. Its chapters began as addresses in evangelistic services. Many people were kind enough to say that the ideas, content and presentation ought to be in print. At first I was reluctant to respond, for reasons set out below, but as more people have made the request it seemed right to explore the possibility. John Stacey of Epworth Press has kindly made it a reality.

Who is this book for? I believe there are many Christians who have a personal faith but who feel themselves to be inadequately informed about the evidence on which faith rests and are therefore reluctant to give reasons for believing. They feel nervous about fellowship within the church where they are encouraged to share their faith. They are even more uneasy about being called to explain their faith to people outside the church. The chapters which follow are offered as a response to that need, a need which is being increasingly expressed by church members.

The other group I have tried to keep in mind are those who seriously wish to consider the Christian faith, but who are puzzled about what lies at its heart. Is it 'whistling in the dark', 'believing in spite of the evidence', 'subscribing to incredible doctrines', or 'accepting a strait-jacket of pre-packaged moral rules'? Or are there grounds for committing one's life to Christ which, though offering neither cast-iron proof (which would remove the need for faith anyway) nor a mystery-free basis for life, do nevertheless make it reasonable to be a Christian today? I have tried to show that there are.

Why then is this book offered so reluctantly? My first reason is that the subject is so profound and means so much to me that I know I will fail to do it justice. I hope I may be forgiven for trying. My second reason for hesitation is that a series of talks will always read like a series of talks, however much one tries to tidy up the style. Yet the speaking manner also requires a certain directness, even colloquialism, and I hope these elements remain. But if readers prefer a fairly refined literary style they would do well to avoid this book.

I suspect that most of all I am aware – as one who has spent most of his ministry teaching in theological colleges – that there is sparse reference to scholarly questions surrounding the affirmations I make and the biblical texts I use, though the discerning reader will perceive a fair amount between the lines. This absence does not reflect a dismissal of scholarly debate. It springs rather from the fact that the evangelist's task is to present the gospel as he understands it, to paint the basic picture with broad and single strokes, to witness to the faith as he perceives and receives it, and to declare it as clearly and intelligibly as he can. In John Wesley's words, his task is to be able to say 'I offered them Christ'. This I have tried to do.

I am deeply grateful to Mrs Margaret Cramb and Mrs Ruth Peachey who typed the various drafts, and to Bertha my wife for help with proof-reading and the references. To her I owe more than I could ever express.

One final point. Part of the preaching style is to make large use of direct speech. I have tried in places to express major elements in Jesus' teaching by ascribing direct speech. In these cases there are no biblical references for no texts exist. Where a biblical saying of Jesus, or even a colloquialized version of one, is used, the reference is given. The prayers at the end of each chapter are offered for any who wish to use them.

DONALD ENGLISH

1

How Shall We Describe Him?

When I first came home from Nigeria as a missionary, I travelled on my own since my wife had come home a few weeks earlier. When I arrived at Heathrow, I was somewhat surprised to discover how many people were there. The lounge for those who are waiting to greet new people was absolutely packed. For a special occasion they had allowed people up on to the roof of the building as well; they were there in their hundreds. Not having expected anyone to come and greet me, I thought my friends had gone a little over the top! It was only when I got to the terminal building I discovered that they were waiting to greet the Beatles!

But there was no doubt about the excitement in the place. I had come on a very long journey, and yet I could feel the tension of it: something very important was happening. And when we ask the question, 'How shall we describe him?', we are trying to enter into a similar spirit so very long ago in Jerusalem. For the question, 'Who is this?', is a question that was often asked about Jesus. When we ask it today we try to establish a link over nearly two thousand years; try to feel again the excitement of the first question that was asked.

I remember a former President of the Methodist Conference telling me how, on his visit to Palestine, he had found himself having breakfast with his wife quite near to Galilee. He turned and said to her, 'Dear, we're breaking bread by Galilee.' He felt the years pass away.

It seems that wherever Jesus went people said, 'Who is this?'. 'Who is this', they said, 'that even the wind and seas obey him?'[1]

'All the city was moved saying, "Who is this?"', about the man who had the crowd surrounding him as he rode in on a donkey.[2] When he healed the man sick of a wasting disease they said, 'Who is this who speaks blasphemy since God alone can forgive sin?'[3] And in Simon's house when a woman broke an alabaster box of ointment to anoint him, they said, 'Who is this who forgives sin also?'[4] The puzzled Herod, not knowing quite what to make of Jesus, said, 'John I have beheaded – but who is this?'[5] Zaccheus, afraid and lonely, 'climbed a tree seeking to see Jesus, who he was'.[6]

So we couldn't be asking a more relevant question, nor in some ways a more difficult one, for we are the age of all ages who find it difficult to know anything. Sartre has in one of his novels his hero, Roquentin, sitting in the park looking at a tree, and trying to understand 'tree-ness'. And he ends up asking himself, 'how he can insult this beautiful growing thing with the simple name "tree"?'[7] How can the simple word 'tree' describe the age, the colour, the strength, the variety, the brownness, the gnarledness, the spreadedness, the greenness, the lifeness? How dare I look at a thing like that and simply say 'tree'! Then he realizes, 'If I don't understand a tree, how do I understand my friends? If I don't understand my friends, do I understand myself?' And that's a very serious question. For as soon as you start to ask the question, 'How shall we describe him?', you find yourself saying, 'And how shall I describe them? And how shall I describe me?'

A few years ago there was a series of four plays on television called *Talking to a Stranger* – Judi Dench was one of the leading actresses in that series. There was a father, a mother, a son and a daughter in the family, and each play told the same story from the point of view of a different character. They managed to have four plays, each lasting one hour, in which there wasn't a single proper conversation. The four characters filled one hour – there were only the four of them in the play – and they all spoke in different directions, but nobody ever actually spoke to anybody else. There was never a speech and a response which actually met the speech with the response. It ended with the mother of the family taking her own life behind the settee, and as she died the last words of the four plays were her words: 'Won't anybody hold me?'

The tragedy of our age is that we know so much, and we know so little; that we know how to describe so many things, and yet we find it difficult to understand one another and ourselves. The Christian church keeps coming back to this question, 'Who is this? Who is he?', because at the heart of our belief is the idea that somehow Jesus is the clue to all the other questions, and that we shall know better how to answer the question, 'Who am I? Who are you?', if we can answer the question, 'Who is or was he?'

The difficulty, of course, is a difficulty of knowing. How can we know the answer about Jesus? Here we need to think a little about proper knowing. Every way of knowing has to be related to what we want to know. If a scientist wishes to teach you that if you mix this chemical substance with that and heat it, you'll get an explosion, you may say, 'I don't believe that'. He will probably then get the mixture, provide you with a beaker, offer you a Bunsen burner, then ask for ten minutes to get clear. In this way he will probably help you to perform your last experiment. If, on the other hand, you say to the historian, 'I don't believe Julius Caesar ever invaded England', he can't take you to Kent, blow a whistle and bring Julius over the water. Historical knowledge is not like scientific knowledge. It operates on a different basis. It uses different criteria because it is examining different evidence. If you say to a musician, 'I don't think that's good music', he can't use either the chemical or the historical method. He won't say, 'Ah, but look at those lines on the paper – have you ever seen anything as parallel as that! Look how absolutely round those round things are! All those squiggles are exactly the same. And the ink is of highest quality.' A musician doesn't demonstrate truth about music the way the historian talks about history or the chemist about chemistry. Should a psychiatrist say, 'If that person doesn't receive treatment he's going to do some damage to himself within the next six months', he's not moving in the same area as the musician or the historian or the scientist. When the general claims, 'I know my men will follow me to the very death', he's not operating in the same field as any of the others; nor is the husband who says, 'I know I love my wife and I know she loves me.'

Every one of those areas of knowledge is a different area, and therefore requires a different discipline. What is more, you must never use one discipline to seek another kind of knowledge and certainly not to dispel it. If I was taken into the hospital tomorrow and was given the early anaesthetic which makes you pleasantly ready for anything, then was rushed into the operating theatre; and if the surgeon were to say, 'I'm going to remove both kidneys', I think even under the influence of that first anaesthetic, I might be able to say, 'But I didn't think you could live without kidneys!' If he were to say, 'Well, actually, no, scientifically you can't, but last night I was reading a poem which suggested the possibility and you're the first on today's operating list' – I think even under the influence of the first anaesthetic I would beat him to the door of the hospital! For poetry is no way to determine medical matters. A poet isn't moving in the medical field, and certainly I don't want any doctor reading poetry and then operating on me on the strength of decisions reached while doing so.

So how do you know about Jesus? Well that's where the difficulty lies, because we're operating in at least two different areas. There is an historical/literary area; that is, there is something written about something which is alleged to have happened. And there is a very personal area; for the gift of Jesus Christ is said to be more than a matter of head knowledge: it's about responding with your whole self. Therefore the Christian, or the person who's interested in Christianity, who asks the question, 'Who is this?' has got to say 'What actually happened? What did he say? What was the result?' A whole host of questions tumble one after another quite properly and Christians ought, more than anybody else, to want to know the answers to those questions. But it is also possible to know the answers to all those questions and miss Jesus Christ. For Christianity is about the giving of yourself to the one whom you discover. So we're trying as we face this question to bring two things together. We're seeking to bring together a story, a series of stories, which were told and written and have been told and commented on age after age. We're trying to bring together that discipline – the historical/literary discipline – and the personal, individual knowledge of each one of us. There's no way you'll know Jesus without those being brought together. It involves both the awareness of something (someone) to respond to, and the making of a personal response.

A person who can't relate to his own or her own history is a very sad person indeed, but so is a person who is locked up in his or her own history. A balanced person is one who can say, 'That's the history; that's what comes down to me, and this is how I respond to it.' That is precisely what Easter is about. So how shall we describe him? What are we to say about Jesus?

I want to point you first to three things which have been written or said about the stories concerning Jesus. I do so because nowadays questions are raised on television and radio, in academic and in popular religious writings, about whether or not these stories are accurate. Here are three comments by scholars of different viewpoints, who have looked at the stories of Jesus.

'What impresses you is the fact that there is so much information that all points in the same direction, and allows you to infer a character of consistency and integrity.'[8] That is, all these stories told so differently, not always told in the same way, not always told with the same fact, not always put at the same time, nevertheless allow you to 'infer a character of consistency and integrity'.

'That someone so relatively obscure and unspectacular as Jesus was should have attracted so complex, vivid and continuing a response – and one which so many great intellects thought it worth rendering in terms of metaphysics and theology – is itself part of his uniqueness.'[9] Fancy such a remote character causing so many books to be written, so many lectures to be given, so many philosophies to be introduced, so many metaphysical systems to be created, so many theologies to be evolved, and all from such an unpromising beginning!

'The size of a crater usually indicates the force of the explosion.'[10]

Well, then, let's try an experiment. Let's try to ask what story 'they' told about him. As I try to answer the question, I ask you to see how you personally relate to the story that I'm trying to tell.

Do you find it possible to infer a consistent person of integrity? Do you find that the size of the crater does indicate the strength of the explosion? Do you find that there's ground here for such a complexity of response?

Let's ask first of all 'Who was he?' at the human level. He had a body like ours. He was born, he grew, he learnt, he ate, he drank, he slept, he was tired. John Knox wrote, 'Unless it be agreed that he was truly human, it does not greatly matter what else can be said of him.'[11] He was a human being! He had passions like ours – when he saw a hungry multitude, he was sorry for them;[12] when children were being kept away from him, he welcomed them;[13] when he saw Jerusalem going quite in the wrong direction, he wept over it;[14] when they said Lazarus was dead, he cried,[15] when the fig tree wasn't producing fruit, he was surprised and astonished and angered by it;[16] and when he saw a temple being turned into a market, he took a whip and chased the offenders.[17] Of course he had passions like ours.

He had temptations far worse than ours. In the wilderness, it would have been so easy to try a trick or two.[18] In Samaria, it would have been easy to respond to his disciples who said, 'Let's show this lot! We're not going to have them saying "No" to us, master. Let's have a bit of fire and thunder – that'll teach them! All the other villages will accept us if you just burn this one.'[19] Jesus must sometimes have felt just like that. In Gethsemane,[20] he knelt (as we so often do, maybe) with all the better solutions to the problem than the one his heavenly Father had. Then in the end he had to learn to say, 'All right, Father I'll do it.' In the judgment hall,[21] when foolish men were trying to be clever and gave him the opportunity to speak out for himself, how hard not to say something; how hard not to respond with a word that would have burned them. But he simply stayed quiet. Of course he was human! Of course he had passions as we have passions! Of course he had temptations as we have temptations! Of course he had people who drove him just about to despair! His humanity is for all to see.

Yet that part of the story is only a part of the story, for the Gospels tell very much more than that and I want to call in some witnesses. Let's think of the acquaintances he met. Let's think of

John's Gospel as John tells the story of Jesus. John the Baptist says, 'I'm not worthy even to unfasten his shoelaces.'[22] Nicodemus, the man in authority, says, 'You must be a teacher come from God, for nobody can do the things you do except God is with him.'[23] A woman – a rather bad woman I would think because she was allowed to go to the well for water on her own, and they usually went together (she was obviously not acceptable, and since she'd had five husbands and the one she was living with wasn't her husband, the whole picture seems to fit) – she goes running back into the village and says, 'Come, see a man who told me everything I ever did.'[24] A man who could never get into the pool fast enough is healed, and he tells the Jews, 'It was Jesus who made me well.'[25] A man is cured of blindness, and when they say, 'This man' (meaning Jesus) 'is a sinner', he says, 'Well, one thing I do know – I used to be blind and now I can see!'[26] And Jesus did it. Martha and Mary, the two sisters, neither knowing what the other has said to Jesus about Lazarus, their brother who is now dead, both say separately, 'If you'd been here, our brother would not have died.'[27]

Now, what is it these people are trying to say? They're trying to say, 'Even on a casual acquaintance we notice there is something about this person that is not like any other person we have ever seen.' Like Mary in the modern musical, *Jesus Christ Superstar*: 'I don't know how to love him.' There aren't the words just to say what they want to say, but they say, 'I wouldn't even feel myself worthy to unfasten his shoelaces.' 'He came into my life and my life's totally different', as Christians ever since have found themselves saying. 'I was blind and now I can see.' 'He told me everything about myself, and we only talked for half an hour.' They're trying to say, 'There's something a bit special here, something a bit different.'

And what about his enemies? Well, they tried to trick him, of course. They said, 'Is it lawful for a man to divorce his wife?'[28] They knew the law all right, but it was a very difficult one, then as now. 'Why don't your disciples fast?'[29] They said, 'It's a good religious tradition. Why don't your followers do it?' They asked his disciples, 'Why does your Master eat with publicans and sinners.'[30] 'What's the new line on that one?' Jesus, on another occasion like this, turned and said, 'You Pharisees clean the outside of the cup and dish, but inside you are full of greed and wickedness.'[31] He saw straight through the question, to what the motive was behind it. So they began to deride him. 'The Pharisees, who loved money, heard all this and were sneering at Jesus.'[32] They even ascribed his power to the Devil. 'By the power of Beelzebub',[33] they said. 'That's it! We can't deny he's doing things, but let's say it comes from the Devil.'

Then they crucified him. And that perhaps was the greatest testimony they ever paid to him. Can you imagine today a modern criminal being executed in London, let us say, and just as he is about to be hanged, the Archbishops of Canterbury and York and the Bishops of Durham and Lincoln, the Cardinal Archbishop of Westminster, and the Moderator of the Free Churches, all come in stately procession, stand around the gallows and start saying, 'Ha! Ha! Got you! Where are your tricks now, young man? Let's see you get your neck out of that one.' But you say, 'Such responsible people would not lower themselves to do that.' Yet that's what happened to Jesus. When they put him on the cross, the religious leaders stood and wagged their fingers at him, and said, 'He saved others, but he cannot save himself . . .'[34] Why would they do that? Because they couldn't believe it. They couldn't believe that everything they knew of him had somehow come to nothing on the cross. They were so surprised they forgot themselves, tripping over their robes to shake their fists.

Now the disciples said a little more about him. Remember who the disciples were: they were very hardy men of the world – fishermen, tax collectors, politicians – not the people you easily fool. They were fanatical monotheists; they'd been brought up to say, 'The Lord our God, the Lord is One'. And they knew Jesus intimately. They'd seen him when he was alone with his little group; they'd seen him in huge crowds. They'd seen him when things were going marvellously; they'd seen him when he was under threat. They'd seen him fresh; they'd seen him very tired. They'd seen him healing many; they'd seen him lonely and on his own. These people, who were fairly sophisticated people, had watched him carefully. What do they say?

Peter says, 'You are the Christ, the Son of the Living God.'[35] Thomas says, 'My Lord and my God.'[36] Paul, later than the others says, 'Lord what would you have me to do?'[37] They're beginning to break the sound barrier of knowledge of the divine. The acquaintances were saying, 'There's something special, there's something a bit more, there's something we don't altogether understand.' The enemy said, 'We don't like it either but we're going to be rid of it.' The disciples said, 'No, you've got to search for some kind of language better than that. If you want to do justice to the whole thing, you'll have to find new words, words you wouldn't use of anyone else.' They search around in their own Jewish past and they come up with 'the Christ', 'the Son of the Living God', 'my Lord and my God', 'Son of God', 'Son of Man', 'Lord', 'Messiah'. Indeed, in the New Testament, writers use phrases from the Old Testament which were used of God and apply them directly to Jesus.

Now it's possible to say, 'Of course, that's what the acquaintances said, that's what the enemy said, that's what his friends said – but what did he say?' Well, listen to this. When Jesus taught them on the mountain,[38] as Matthew has it, or on the plain, as Luke has it, he claims an authority which no man had ever claimed. Do you remember how he said, 'It was said by them of old times' (or 'to them of old times'), '"Don't do this! Don't do that! Do this! Do that!" But *I* say to you . . . '? That is, he takes what is received as law from God, and he says, 'Now listen to what *I* may say about it.' He takes it, an outer law, and he turns it in on them. 'You've been told not to commit adultery: if you lust it's as good as done.' 'You've been told not to kill your brother: if you despise him you've as good as murdered him.' With all the authority of God, he takes the law and turns it inside out, and says, 'How do you look when I do that to you?' That's an authority no one has ever claimed.

He also assumed the right to forgive sins. There is the story of the man let down through the roof (one of the moments when Jesus was stopped in full flow as a preacher – how hard that must have been! He'd just got to point two and down through the ceiling comes a body! We don't train our preachers to handle that kind of a situation!). The man is lowered down and everyone is looking to see what is going to happen, and they're wondering what Jesus is going to do. He turns to them and says, 'That you may know that the Son of Man has power on earth to forgive sins', and then he says to the man who is ill, 'Rise and walk!'[39] And they're horrified. Not because he's healed him – there were other people doing healing jobs. It was because he said, 'I'm healing him to prove that I can forgive sins.' And the Pharisees rightly said, 'Who forgives sins but God alone?' Quite right. Quite right. Who forgives sins but God alone? Exactly.

He claimed the central place in judgment. He says in John 'This is the condemnation: that light has come into the world and men prefer darkness to light.'[40] 'Many will come unto me and say, "Lord, Lord, did we not do this, that and the other for you?" And I'll say, "I didn't know you. Who are you?"'[41] He claims the right to a person's total allegiance. People come and say, 'Lord, we'll be ready to follow you in about a week's time. I think I could get all my affairs cleared up in about a week's time – and, of course, I have to tell the wife.' Jesus says, 'No, no, that's all right, don't bother. If you can't come now, don't come.' How harsh. How hard. But you see, he's wanting them to know that when he calls, it means everything. Everything's included. And so he won't allow any way of making an excuse. 'No man having put his hand to the plough and turning back is fit for the Kingdom of God.'[42] 'If any man comes unto me, and hates not father, mother, wife, brothers, sisters, children, houses, lands – yes, and his own life also – he cannot be my disciple.'[43] How hard! But Jesus is saying, 'It's all right, bring them all! I'll look after them. Give them to me, because I demand total allegiance.' His hardest demand turns out to be his kindest offer – 'The more of your life you give me, the more of your life I'll be able to care for and enrich.'

He claims a unique relationship with his Father. 'I and the Father are one,' he said.[44] Philip said, 'Lord, show us the way. We just want the way!' 'Philip, have I been all this time with you and you haven't seen yet? I *am* the way, I *am* the truth, I *am* the life.'[45] Can you believe that a man would say that, with all the meaning of way and truth and life coming out of the Jewish background? 'I am *it*, Philip.'[46] And once John records him as saying, 'Which of you convicts me of sin?'[47] To crowds, to enemies, to friends, he offers the chance to point out anything wrong with his life. As far as we can tell, no one took up the offer.

Now, this is the story. This is what comes down to us. And you can't get rid of it by cutting a few verses out here and there. The difficulty with the things Jesus says is that he said them so many times. And he said the things we don't care for too much alongside the things we quite like. For example, it is good to accept his words 'Whoever believes in the Son has eternal life'.[48] The difficulty is that the sentence, as John records it, continues, 'Whoever disobeys the Son will not have life, but will remain under God's judgment.' That's less easy to take. Yet it's not easy to cut half a verse out. (I know, of course, he didn't speak in verses!) But, you see, you can't take half of it and say, 'Now that's probably what he said, and we'll just forget the other bit.' For these claims either stand or they fall all together.

I've tried hard to make sense of those who look at Jesus and make him other than what the Christian church makes him out to be. I had a time at university when I struggled very deeply with that; when I wondered whether he could be what the Christians said he was. And I have to say, with all the honesty I can summon up, I am not gullible enough to believe that he was anything other than the Son of God. I can't bring myself to believe that this story points other than to one who is human, who is with us, who is alongside us, and yet who, all the time he's alongside us, is God's own revelation of himself in a way which makes him also different from us. If you find that hard to hold together, so do I, and so do most Christians. This is why I talk about bringing the historical/literary method alongside the personal method. There are many things in life one doesn't understand, yet which we take on trust and test them out. And the testimony of Christians is that when you take him as the story reveals him and trust your life to him he turns out to be what he claims to be.

Now I want to ask one last set of questions because I believe they trouble some people. 'It's all right to say', one argument goes, 'that he lived in our world – of course I'm ready to accept that.' Those who have seriously studied Scripture as professionals have asked very many very serious questions about Jesus

Christ and I don't want to devalue that at all. But none of them, as far as I know, has ever reached the conclusion on the basis of such rigorous study that Jesus didn't actually live. So people say, 'Yes, he lived in our world but wasn't it a very different world from ours? So how can he have much to do with us?' Well, I ask you to make a simple distinction between culture and nature. Nature includes the fact that we eat: culture is whether we eat with our fingers or with a knife and fork. Nature is men and women being attracted to one another: culture is the kind of wife you look for. One of my Nigerian friends once said to me, 'Why do you Westerners go for the skinny fair ones?' He'd been looking at posters of film stars, you see, and in that era they were mostly of the Betty Grable/Marilyn Monroe type. What he meant was that in Nigeria they had a much more sensible view which was that you should choose a wife who was fairly well-built for work and child-bearing. Now do you see: he wasn't saying it was wrong to have a woman – that's nature, if you like – but culture is what kind of wife you choose. Now I ask you to ponder that very seriously. Of course Jesus didn't ever fly in an aeroplane. Of course Jesus didn't have to learn how to operate a computer. (I'm jealous of him for that!) Of course he didn't. But is life really (pardon me, those of you who live by computers), but does life really consist of the abundance of computerability a man possesses?! No, life is about relationships, it's about being born, it's about growing up, it's about loving, sometimes it's about hating, it's about helping, it's about being hurt, it's about being ill and about being healthy, it's about being happy or unhappy, joyful or not joyful, and so on. Those are things that life is really about, and those things are nature, not culture. The shape of them may change from generation to generation but the reality of them does not, and Jesus knew all about all of that.

Others may say, 'Yes, but don't Christians say that he was sinless? You see, that's the big difference, isn't it? – because if he was sinless then he doesn't actually know what it's like to be us, does he?' No, he doesn't; and he doesn't for a very good reason: that we fall into sin when temptation gets to be too much, but he never did. He plumbed temptation to its very depths by never giving in. If I had to fight the world heavyweight boxing champion, I would simply hope that in the very first minute he'd hit me good and hard, and that would be the end of that. But supposing I could fight him for fifteen rounds. Supposing when we got to the fifteenth round and up towards about the fifteenth second from the end I was able to say to him, 'Anything else you'd like to say? Any other way you'd like to hit me . . ?' And then supposing when we got to eleven seconds to go I was just able to land one, right on his jaw, and knock him flat out! I think I might from time to time at social gatherings say, 'Did I ever tell you about the time I . . . ' – and I'd have the right to! For I would have exhausted the great World Champion! And people would want to say, 'What happened when he said this? What happened when he hit you?' Now, no one who had ever been knocked out by him would be able to understand what I had gone through because they succumbed before the full range of punches were used. But I would have borne them all and still survived.

In the same way none of us who falls into sin knows what it's like to feel temptation to the very depths of its possibilities and never give in. And our Lord is different from us in that, and necessarily so. Because, however deeply we are tempted – and some of us undergo very, very deep temptations indeed – no matter how deeply we're tempted, and how it hurts and almost destroys us, Jesus is always able to say, 'I've been further than this. I know what this is like. And I can stand by you here, even if it gets worse, I've still always been further down the road!' That to me is what makes Jesus so much more wonderful than anybody else! He's always a little way ahead. In the darkest place, he's always saying, 'It's all right – if you look down you'll see some footsteps. I've been there already.'

'Ah, but', we say, 'you see, that means that he's not identical to us, is he? Because he doesn't start against temptation with a bad record.' Well, no, he doesn't. But if I was off the end of the pier drowning and somebody dropped in beside me and said, 'I can't swim either, but I thought you'd like company,' I might be impressed for a little while . .! I can't say I'd be greatly helped. I need some great brawny chap who's got all his badges tattooed on his arm! – who says, 'It doesn't matter which way you go, we'll have you straight to the shore.' That's what I need when I'm drowning: and that's what Jesus is! The man who drops in beside me, facing the huge waves which are killing me, but who can swim, is identifying himself wholly with me. That's what I need. It's no good him dropping in at the children's paddling pool saying, 'If you had been drowning here, I could have helped you.' I need him off the end of the pier *now*! If he drops in there, right where the water is worst and says, 'I'll come and save you', that's identification. And that, I think, is what Jesus did for us.

He became identified with us; and becoming identified with us, he showed us what God was like in a very special way, because – as John says at the opening of his Gospel – he is the word of creation. He's the one who is the clue to the whole created life. He's not just the clue to the church – that's much too narrow – he's the clue to everything. Life is only properly understood in Jesus Christ, for he is the word of creation who was made flesh and dwelt among us. He revealed God in a very special way and he pointed to life's deepest qualities. How much do you love? How much do you trust? How clean are you inwardly in your thinking processes, in your attitudes? How perceptive are you of what God is doing in his world? How broad is your vision of what life is about in the light of eternity? That's what Jesus talked about. And in talking about these things, he dealt with the very problems that were there in the first century and are still with us now: the flaming rows in families; the jealousy of one to another; the harshness of one brother to another brother; the lack of sympathy of authorities in relation to workers; the ways in which people maltreat one another and the created world; our capacity for doing wrong but refusing to admit that we're wrong; the way in which we'd rather blame somebody else than admit that it was our fault. Even when we know we've been hurt and we know we've hurt others, we say, 'She can come first – I'll be here. I don't mind considering an apology.' That's where Jesus was operating.

When his world was saying, 'It's wrong to do this', Jesus was saying, 'It's wrong to think it.' When his contemporaries said, 'There's a law for that', Jesus said, 'What about that for which there is no law – what you think and feel yourself?' And when people were saying, 'Make sure your public image is right', Jesus was replying 'I've got an X-ray machine that sees right to the very heart of your being and you don't fool me, and you don't fool my heavenly Father.' Whether that's twentieth century or fifteenth century or first century, it's what it's about. He revealed the deep problems that we have, the ways in which we offend one another. And if we offend one another, how does it feel to God? If we're offending fellow human beings, what does the Creator make of it, I wonder? Oh, how necessary it is for us to be right with him! And that we might be right with him, Jesus took this loving approach right to the very end and he said, 'I'll die for this. My heavenly Father so loves you and wants you, that I'm going to show you how much he loves you.' Even when those who ought to have known better handed him over to others who couldn't have known better, who put him to death, Jesus still went on that way, for it was the way of love. And when God raised him from the dead, he was announcing that even death isn't the end, because we have a much wider and broader perspective than that.

And so Jesus keeps popping up in history. Just when one bit of culture seems to have got rid of him, up he comes somewhere else. I travel around this country, and people keep asking me about the Methodist decline in membership, and so I tell them about Korea: the largest Christian church in the world – 23,000 members in one church! The largest Methodist church in the world – 10,000 members in one Methodist church, all of them meeting in classes. All the class leaders meet every week and the minister instructs them and then off they go and instruct the classes. They have services at 9.00 and 10.00 and 11.00 and 12.00 on Sundays just to get everybody in!

He still calls people to be disciples. He still invites us to say, 'I want to put this history together with my present experience. I want to say about that story which has come down to me, "Yes, yes, yes – yes, I want to know this inner purity that at the moment eludes me. Yes, I want to be right with God. I want to stop fooling around. I want to stop making believe I'm a Christian. I want really to give myself to him. Yes, there are particular things which I need to confess to God and get right. Yes, there are relationships that need putting right. Yes, it's time I stopped playing at half-Christianity and become a full Christian."' Jesus invites us in. And that brings us right back to where we started: with the crowds on Palm Sunday shouting, 'Hosanna!' Jesus invites us not to watch the play, but to join in.

This understanding of Jesus poses questions for all of us. For those who are committed to Jesus Christ, there is the possibility that some things in our lives need to be put right. Maybe we have slipped away, and although the outward performance looks the same, the inner part of it has really just about gone? There is no better time than now. Maybe some who read know that they are not Christians; have never committed themselves to him. Maybe there's one particular thing that holds you back, and you now see why, being loved like this, you'd really be much better to give it up. Maybe some have never been Christians, but have already come too far down the road now not to be a Christian. Well, why don't you? Why bother walking all the way back again? If you've come so far, come in! There's plenty of room for everybody.

Paul says, 'He is the Son of God who loved me and gave himself for me.'[49] Every one of us can make that our own story. 'The Son of God', not just a human being, God and man – that's the only way to make sense of the evidence. 'The Son of God, who loved me' – loved enough to come to earth, loved enough to teach and heal, loved enough to die, loved enough to rise from the dead. 'The Son of God who loved *me*'! Fancy that! So long ago, so far away, and yet his love was for me as much as it was for everybody else.

'Help us, Father, to be able to discern between the words of others and your words to us. Give us courage, Lord, we who have had the privilege of hearing your voice, not to turn away from it. If we have built up years of resistance against you and your love is melting that resistance down, give us grace, Lord, to thank you and to give ourselves. If we are Christians who are not walking properly with you and need to get right with you; Lord, give us grace to turn again and face you, and be welcomed by you. If we are Christians who've slipped right away, and need to be restored to the family; Lord, thank you that you love us all the same. Give us grace to make our way back, and help us, every one, who have read the story of Jesus again, felt him living amongst us; help us to open our arms, to open our hearts and our minds to your love, that you may be at home in our hearts. Give us courage and grace, Lord, so to do. We ask it in the name of Jesus Christ, the Son of God, the Saviour of the world, and our Lord. Amen.'

2

What Did He Teach?

I watched with great fascination a television programme on soccer violence – that is, violence on the terraces of our football grounds. I could hardly believe my eyes or my ears when I saw one supporter setting out the philosophy of the soccer hooligan. It was quite clearly thought out. He said, 'We go with the club's honour at stake. We go to other people's football grounds . . .', and the interviewer interrupted and said, 'Well, that's all right. They provide a space for you.' 'Ah!' he said, 'that's no good. It's no good unless you take the *home* supporters' ground. You've got to go into the place where they are.' And the interviewer said, 'Why?' 'Well', he said, 'what would they think of our club if we don't take the home supporters' end?' The whole philosophy of the football hooligan was there. Everything stood or fell by being able to 'take' the home supporters' enclosure. That gave meaning to me, I have to say, for much that happens: the scarves and the hats; the various ways of drawing attention to ourselves, to the team; the sense of security we have in relating to things like that; the reason why some people have had their ashes scattered on Liverpool Football Ground; why people have named their family after an entire football team. It's a search for some way in which we say, 'This is where my identity is. This is where I find my security.'

So it doesn't surprise me that three great philosophies in our day have attracted great support. Humanism says there is no outside help beyond human history and achievement. You have only what you receive from your tradition and what you and your fellow human beings are able to do. So you should seek all the happiness you can without any help from outside. There isn't a lot of happiness about. Humanism has lots of followers.

Or there is existentialism with its sense of meaning or meaninglessness. In determination first to get at what meaning is about and then to authenticate oneself, one should act and behave in a way which is self-authenticating. It is wrong to worry about ultimate meanings because you have to make decisions all the time without adequate information. There is not a lot of professional existentialism on the factory floor or in the home, but there's an awful lot of living without concern for meaning, and it's pretty much the same.

Communism reflects deep concern to share the resources of the world fairly, with an economic clue to the process by which this has been destroyed and therefore the process by which it will be built up. In a world where so many resources are controlled by so few, and where so many people are exploited and underprivileged, it is not surprising that many turn to Communism where their needs are taken seriously and a solution offered. Christians do well to take very seriously the enormous support for humanism, existentialism and communism in the world, and that's why we should ask ourselves about what Jesus actually taught.

It is also important because we often seem to get it wrong. We treat the teaching of Jesus like a set of rules which have reluctantly to be obeyed because it's the only way to get into the Kingdom. Rather like that Jewish story which sees the commandments coming, not by God giving them to Moses, but by Moses negotiating them with God. And at one break in the negotiations, Moses comes down from the mountain and says, 'I've got him down to ten, but I'm afraid adultery is still in.'

Now Jesus's way of teaching was not actually the way of giving a law. Jesus's way of teaching was to talk about the Kingdom, and the moment he mentioned the Kingdom, the Kingdom of God or the Kingdom of Heaven, every Jewish listener was pretty sure he knew what he was talking about. After all, they'd been waiting for generations for the Kingdom to be restored. They wanted a firm control. They wanted a strong political system. They wanted an army that could first of all overthrow Rome and then defeat the nations round about and restore the time of David. So when they heard him talk about the 'Kingdom' they were pretty sure they knew what he was about.

What his hearers were to discover was that, in fact, the Kingdom which Jesus spoke about was very different from anything they expected. For example, it was a very surprising kind of Kingdom. It wasn't so much a realm (that is, an area over which somebody ruled), it was more the *fact* that God ruled. He declared, 'The Kingdom is at hand, so repent and believe the Gospel.' That is, he did not say, 'The Kingdom is where Jews are.' He did not say, 'The Kingdom is Palestine and wherever we can extend.' He said, 'The Kingdom is wherever men and women have learned first of all to find fault with themselves, to repent, and then to believe in the Kingdom – to put their trust somewhere.' That is, the Kingdom was for Jesus a very interior experience. It was a case of learning to put God first.

Putting God first for Jesus meant relating to God through him. Jesus said, 'If I, by the Spirit of God, cast out demons, then the Kingdom of God has come among you.'[1] Looking out from where he stood in the middle of them, he said, 'The Kingdom of God is in the midst of you.'[2] It was no longer a matter of extending a physical realm; it was a matter of saying, 'The Kingdom is about inner relationships with God, and I am at the heart of those.' Emil Bruner wrote, 'He does not turn men away from his person. He binds them precisely to himself and regards the decision which is made in his presence as one which is made in the presence of God himself. The coming Kingdom is present only in him.' What a surprise that was for Jesus' audience who thought the Kingdom was about an earthly realm, with an earthly government, with an earthly king, extending its power. It was about inwardness. It was about how you relate inwardly to God of all creation. It was about whether you have managed to discover that proper relationship in Jesus Christ. It was a relationship which would produce character. That's why he taught the beatitudes: 'Blessed are the poor in spirit . . . ' and so on. While they were concentrating on outward deeds, on keeping laws, on getting the practice right, getting the ritual right, he was saying, 'It's character I'm talking about. The

Kingdom is about so being inwardly related to God through me, that character is developed.'

I have a friend who, after a disastrous French examination paper when she was an undergraduate, wrote, 'Some of my friends think I'm quite beautiful.' She was drawing attention to the fact that there are more things in the world than good examination answers! Jesus was drawing attention away from the laws and asking about the inner state of people. So the Kingdom came as a surprise to his hearers.

Jesus spelt out five different things about the Kingdom which really are at the heart of his ministry. He taught them all in the parables which are, after all, one third of all his teaching. He tried to help them through the parables to hear what the Kingdom was about, and the parable is meant to gather you into itself. Günther Bornkamm wrote, 'The parables deny the hearer the role of the spectator.'[3] Jeremias wrote, 'The parables of Jesus compel his hearers to come to a decision about his person and mission.'[4]

We had in another church where we used to worship a missionary evening on 'Poverty and Hunger in the World'. Everyone bought a ticket for a meal, but when the people who'd bought the tickets got there, about thirty were served a full meal on the platform. The rest were given bread and cheese down on ground floor level. There was an involvement in the problem of hunger that night such as we had never before seen in our church! The people sitting at the high table could hardly eat the food as all the hungry sat watching them. Soup . . . main course . . . sweet – while the rest tried to make their bread and cheese last out until the talk came. The parable is like that. You go along all innocently to hear it, but as you listen Jesus uses the parable to draw you into the story until you are making decisions yourself.

These are the five things which emerge from the parables which are at the centre of the teaching of Jesus:

The Kingdom is about something entirely new, not about doctoring the old. Jesus told the parable of the old and the new wine skins; of the old wine skins that couldn't hold the new wine because new wine requires new wine skins, and bursts the old.[5] He was trying to help them to see that there is all the difference in the world between religion and Christianity. There is all the difference in the world between a system through which you go, observing the things to be done and doing them, altering them a little here and a little there if they don't quite suit; and this relationship with God of an interior kind. 'To be brought up in the system', Jesus was saying, 'will not make you a follower of mine.' Or, as Billy Graham put it more simply, 'If you're born in a garage, that doesn't make you a motor car.' You see, it's not about saying, 'I learnt this here and that there. I was taught to do this in this way and that in that way – sometimes I change it around a little.' Jesus says, 'No, no, no – it's about an inward thing, an inner revolution', which (when he talked to Nicodemus) he called 'new birth'.

So the first question Jesus was putting to his hearers was not, 'Do you know the routine?'; or, 'Are you at home in a place of worship?'; or, 'Do you understand the history of our religion?' The first question he was putting was 'Has this new, effervescent experience of the inwardness of God's love actually reached inside you? Or are you still trying to move along with the old way?'

The second point about the Kingdom is that it is a gift. He told a story about some vineyard workers.[6] Those who worked one hour were paid the same wage as those who'd done a full shift. Doesn't that make you angry? Don't you keep on wanting to say, 'Yes, but, just a minute . . .' You could hardly introduce it into one of our current management/labour disputes as a guiding principle. You see, that's actually not what it's about. They are parables of the Kingdom. And so you have to say to yourself, 'Why do I get angry? What is it that causes me to want to say "Hey, just a minute, why are they getting the same as them? It isn't fair, is it?"' Jesus says, 'No, precisely; it is not fair. Not if you want to work on a basis of owning and earning what you deserve. If you want what you deserve, we can operate like that, but don't expect much.' As the man said when the boss claimed, 'I pay you what you're worth', the employee replied, 'I don't want what I'm worth, I want enough to live on!' You see, Jesus is saying, 'My Father is a gracious God.' He doesn't ask you to earn salvation. He's not asking you to work it out for yourself. He's offering you something.

When the vineyard owner says 'Am I not free to be gracious? Am I not free to give as I want to?' he's echoing the very voice of God himself. For this parable is a parable of the Kingdom which says,'Not only do you not need to earn your salvation – you couldn't if you tried – it's God's free gift.'

I have a friend who finds it very difficult to receive any gift. She really is genuinely embarrassed when you give her anything, and one of the hardest things in her Christian life has been to receive the bread and wine of Holy Communion. Somebody, somewhere down the line, has filled her with this sense that she's got to be worthy, and she never feels worthy. There's the story of the tent evangelist who used to take his tent around the country, preaching as he went. He went into one village and put his tent up and laid the seats and the hymn books out, and started his mission. One young man sat in the back of the meeting every night and had a whale of a time! He laughed and he giggled; he made *sotto voce* comments which everybody could hear; when anything was said which wasn't quite right, he made the most of it; and, night after night, he ruined the meetings. The evangelist used to dread seeing this young man there, but he was there every night. When the last night was over, and it had gone pretty much in the same way, the evangelist started picking up the hymn books. To his amazement, the young man didn't move – he stayed at the back. As the evangelist got nearer, picking up the hymn books, the young man came to him. He said, 'I've ruined your meetings this week, haven't I?' 'Well, yes', said the evangelist, 'you have.' 'But', he said, 'I listened tonight, and I want you to tell me what can I do to be a Christian?' The evangelist just kept on picking up books and said 'You're too late' and walked away. The young man followed him along the row, picking up the hymn books as he went. 'No', he said, 'it's not a joke. I really do mean it. What I can do to be a Christian.' The evangelist just said, 'You're too late' and picked up another whole row of books. When they got right to the back, the young man got hold of him and said, 'I'm not going to go until you tell me! I'm sorry! I've done the wrong thing. What can I do to be a Christian?' And the evangelist turned and said, 'You're too late: Jesus has done everything to make it possible for you to be a

Christian. Just accept what he's offered.' Most of Jesus' hearers found that so hard to believe and accept! And so do we. In our need for a personal knowledge of God, and for a sense of forgiveness for what is wrong in our lives, in our search for meaning in life, and for power to live with integrity, it isn't easy to accept that Jesus Christ's life, death and resurrection provide all the foundation we need. There's an old hymn which says, 'There is a fountain filled with blood, drawn from Emmanuel's veins, and sinners plunged beneath that flood lose all their guilty stains.' It's a rather old-fashioned hymn, but it has a very modern ring to it.

If only we can learn that the Kingdom is not about earning your long-service certificate! It's not about getting enough premiums on the insurance that when you get to heaven Peter will let you in! It's not simply about being able to say, 'I was a good citizen, a good father, a good mother, a good child, a good workman, a good . . . ' It's about learning that if we tried from now to eternity we couldn't earn the forgiveness which God offers. We couldn't merit the love which he allows to flow out to us. Jesus tells the story of the vineyard labourers to make the point. When we are beginning to get all excited about the story, and say, 'But that isn't fair!' Jesus is saying, 'Yes, you should be glad it isn't, because my heavenly Father offers you everything you need.' 'You couldn't deserve the new start he offers: why not be humble enough to accept it?'

The third thing about the Kingdom is that anybody may belong to it. Another of Jesus' stories is about a prodigal son and his older brother.[7] The boy took all his inheritance early and wasted it. He came back later – greatly disillusioned and apologetic – with his speech ready. Not only did he not get through his speech, however; he found his father waiting, looking, watching. When the son made his way up the road and started to speak, 'Father, I've sinned against heaven and against you . . . ' – he'd been rehearsing it all the way – 'Father, I've sinned against heaven and against you, and am no more worthy . . . ' 'Yes, yes, yes,' said his father, 'Lovely. Thank you. Come on in, let's have a party!' 'But I haven't finished my speech!' 'You're welcome. You were dead, and you're alive again!' The story of the Kingdom is the story of God's unfailing love offered openly and endlessly to us. It's the story which says it doesn't matter what you've been, it doesn't matter where you've been, it doesn't matter what you've done. Can he really mean this? It doesn't matter how unworthy you are, it doesn't matter how wrong you've been, it doesn't matter how good you've been, how goody-goody you've been! It doesn't matter that everyone else is saying 'She'd never need to be saved – she's so lovely.' 'He's so good – he won't need the Kingdom.' Jesus says we all need the Kingdom; if only by his grace we can see our need for him and come.

There is a man in the Church of Scotland ministry now who is a former murderer. The shock that went through the Church of Scotland when that was announced! But why not? I know a vicar in England who served for many years in a particular parish. Then one night they were giving testimony, and he told of his years in prison. It was a lovely, rather expensive, suburban area: some of the congregation took a long time to recover from that! He'd never told them that he was a former prisoner. But the Kingdom is for all who will come, as the prodigal came saying, 'I'm sorry. I'm not worthy. I'll do anything you ask me to do, if only you'll let me in.' The father simply said, 'Welcome back! It's party-time!'

The fourth thing in the parables of Jesus is that it costs nothing – and yet it costs everything. As somebody put it, 'The entrance fee is nothing, but the annual fee is everything.' Jesus told another story when large crowds were following him. (If in the Gospels you come across, 'Large crowds were following him' – look out! The next thing is going to be a fairly shocking statement. It's as though the disciples tried to gather the crowds together, and Jesus tried to disperse them! For as they came in large crowds, as he became more popular, then he got down to what the Kingdom was really about.) Large crowds were travelling with Jesus (says Luke)[8] and turning to them he said, 'If anyone comes to me and does not hate his father and mother, his wife and children, his brothers and sisters – yes, even his own life', chorus: 'he cannot be my disciple.' 'Anyone who does not carry his cross and follow me', chorus: 'cannot be my disciple.' 'Any of you who does not give everything he has', chorus:

'cannot be my disciple.' In between those sayings, we have the story of the foolish king and the foolish builder. The king who, one day, got up and said, 'I think we'll have a war today', sent off his troops to fight. But as they moved they discovered the enemy had twice as many soldiers. So they sent back a messenger who said, 'King, are you sure today's the day for the war? They've got twice as many soldiers.' 'Oh', he said, 'it mustn't be then. I must have made a mistake. I'll send ambassadors.' So the ambassadors went and said to the other king, 'So sorry. It's all an administrative mistake. We didn't intend war really. We really wanted peace. We just got it wrong.' And Jesus says to the crowd, 'Which of you would do that?' The Greek construction expects the answer, 'Not likely!' 'No sir, not me!'

Jesus told of a man who thought one day, 'I'll build a tower.' He didn't look at his books; just started to build his tower. When he got halfway up, the workmen came and said, 'We need more bricks.' 'Oh, well', he said, 'we haven't any money.' 'Well', they said, 'we can't build then.' 'Oh!' So ever after that in the village, people said, 'Old so-and-so's folly – do you see it, over there? He actually started building without counting the cost!' And Jesus's question is, 'Which of you would?' But the answer is, 'Not likely! Not me! I'd never make a mistake like that.' 'Well then', Jesus says, 'don't, don't. Don't start being my disciple if you're not willing to give it everything.' The Kingdom costs nothing – it's given freely – and yet it invites you to give everything: father, mother, wife, children, brothers, sisters, houses, lands, your life, your possessions. 'Everything', he says, 'I'm asking.' You see, he's using an accountancy model. He's saying, 'I'm not talking about income and expenditure. I'm not saying how much have you got now? – give me that. I'm talking about the budget. I'm asking whether you're willing to budget everything. I'm asking whether you're willing actually to have only one account marked "For Jesus Christ". I'm asking you to budget everything you know and everything that might be. And I'm asking you to budget all for me.'

I spoke on this passage in the south of Nigeria at a conference of missionaries and we stayed with the secretary of the mission.

His wife was expecting a baby. Through the night she lost her baby. I was very upset, as my wife was, because we feared that the business of getting ready for us might have caused unnecessary work for her. I went to see her in the little hospital there at the mission station. I said, 'I'm awfully sorry if anything we've done has caused you this unhappiness.' She looked me straight in the face and said, 'I'd budgeted for this.' She'd heard me the night before and she understood the talk better than I did. 'I'd budgeted for it.' Because, you see, what seems like a very hard saying of Jesus is, in fact, one of the kindest things he ever said. For what he's saying is: 'If you will put into my care, if you will give into my keeping, every area of your life – your relationships, your ambition, what you hope to be, what matters most to you – if you will put all these things into my hands, then that which is best for you will be enriched, and that which is not good for you will simply fall away.' Once everything is into his hands, then you really are free, because now you've grasped that there's only one absolute demand on your life, and that's God's demand in Jesus. Every other demand is relative, whether it's of family, or work, or ambition, or culture, or whatever it is, it's all relative now to the one demand which Jesus makes, which is the demand of the one who loves us.

If only we could learn that. When, in his presence, maybe as we do now, we feel uneasy about some habits in our lives, and we clutch them to ourselves rather than handing them over, his love is saying, 'But, don't you see, without them you'd be so much better?' Or when we clutch relationships that are perfectly fine, he simply wants them in order that he might refine them and, within his own context, make them what they might be. But we want to hold them for ourselves: 'You're not having this!' He says, 'Well, all right, but it'll rot. It'll be like the second lot of manna that you didn't need. It'll go rotten on you.' When we say, 'I don't want to hand over my future because I don't know what it will be.' 'All right, but you won't pick the best way yourself.' When we want to hold on to friendships that are actually spoiling our Christian lives: 'All right, but it will be worse, not better.' If only we can learn what it means to give everything into his hands.

I knew a man whose whole personal life was in chaos. He came to talk to me about it. And the trouble with him was he wanted to control everything. He wanted to control everybody at work; he wanted to control everybody at home; he wanted to control every relationship into which he came. Bit by bit, everything he tried to control turned against him. By the time he got to me, everything was just about in ruins. It was only as he began to grasp that what he clutched he lost, and what he freely gave to the Lord he gained, that he entered into anything like freedom. There in my study he knelt and gave his life and everything else into the hands of Christ. It is when we clutch things to ourselves that our lives are spoiled.

It costs nothing, for he welcomes us freely, but love takes all, for love wants to care for all.

The fifth thing in the teaching of Jesus is that it is the most important decision of all. Jesus told the story of a rich fool.[9] This man realized how well he was doing in farming, so decided to pull down his present barns and build larger. Then he sat down alone to give himself a party! He could give only himself a party because there was nobody else there. And, Jesus says, that night the voice came: 'You idiot! Tonight your soul is required of you. And what's all this going to do for you now?' It's like a man being burned to death in his own house because he wouldn't leave his gold. Jesus keeps on bringing crisis into people's lives. They go to listen to a little story – they come away absolutely disturbed. Because, when they listen to him, they suddenly realize that this is the most important decision they'll ever make. It is the same for us. Decisions about work, decisions about career, decisions about marriage, decisions about where we live, which countries we'll go to, these decisions are *minor* decisions compared with the decision about eternity: about whether our lives will be open to God or whether they will not be open to God. And Jesus's teaching about the Kingdom is based, fairly and squarely, there.

And so I have, as a Christian writer, to remind you that two kingdoms are available: the Kingdom of this world, in which you can achieve a lot and be a very respectable and respected person, or the Kingdom of our Lord Jesus Christ, which is a new thing, not a patched up old thing. It's not 'religion'; it's a lively faith. It is available freely because God in Jesus Christ died and rose again to declare the quality of his love. It is available for all, for anyone who wishes may belong to the Kingdom. It is offered on the basis of love, which means that it wishes to embrace you altogether. Every part of your life, now and in the future, is possessed by the Lord Jesus Christ when you give yourself to him. And it is the most important decision you will ever make.

Please don't misunderstand me. I'm not saying that everyone who becomes a Christian becomes a Christian by a sudden decision. Some people are salvaged in that way, others are cultivated. Some can never remember a moment when they did not believe in the Lord Jesus Christ. Others know now they do not believe in the Lord Jesus Christ in this sense in which he spoke. I am not making a distinction between those two, and saying that one is right and the other is wrong – that's totally unbiblical. The question is not whether you grew to love him and serve him, or whether you came at a given moment to him. The question is whether you do love him and serve him or not.

Maybe some reading this have never entered into what I'm talking about. It's all a strange world to you because you don't understand it. Maybe there are those who belong to Jesus Christ and who understand only too well what I am describing, and have felt more and more uncomfortable as the chapter has gone on, for you belong to him but you are holding back things from him. Maybe there are areas of life which resist his presence; new areas he wishes to develop which you will not allow; things which you know to be wrong in your life which are spoiling your Christian discipleship. And maybe there are still others who are Christians who are being called forward and have got stuck.

I want to say the same thing to all of us, whatever our condition. Paul said that he believed in the Son of God who loved him and gave himself for him. The offer of the Kingdom, which is centred in the teaching of Jesus, is made possible through the love of Jesus. That love was demonstrated once for all when he gave his life for us on the cross and rose again. Therefore, if he touches our life and says, 'You have not yet ever given yourself to me', we have nothing to be afraid of. They are the arms of divine love which reach out to hold us. Why should we hold back any longer? If we are Christians who've been half-hearted about our service, holding back things lest it should not be the best for us: why would hands marked with the sign of the nails of the cross take you to where you ought not to be? Why would the Son of God, who loves you enough to give himself for you, take you anywhere that is not the very best for you? Why hold from him things which, when they're put into his hands, will either be enriched or will go because they're not the best for us? Why hold anything back from him who loves us like that? And if he is calling us as Christians to service from which we have turned away: why do we turn away from eternal love? He offers himself in order to enrich us to the full.

Jesus's words were and are, 'The Kingdom of God is at hand. Repent', that is, turn away from what you've been, 'and believe the Gospel.'

When I went first to the United States, I saw something which I found to be both moving and effective. It's what the Americans call 'an alter call', and I found it a very attractive and a very simple thing. When I'd finished speaking I sat down and someone else took over who understood the people and the language. The altar call was simply the offer given to anyone present in the church to come to the rail during the singing of a hymn, and to kneel or to stand, and then, if they wished, having made their commitment, just to go back to their places. I thought it was a rather lovely thing. Some stayed on because they were making a new commitment to Christ and they needed some help. Others stayed on because the matter about which they were troubled as Christians required some advice and there were people trained to help them. Others simply had something they wanted to get right on their own with the Lord, and they came to the rail and knelt or stood just to say publicly in the House of God, 'Lord, I want to get this settled now.' Then they went quietly back to their places – nobody counselled them, nobody troubled them – they'd done what they wanted to do. That seemed to me to be a very nice and open way to respond to what God says.

You don't need an altar call in a church, of course, though many have found such a public commitment helpful. God is available anywhere – now – for our prayerful commitment of ourselves to be a reality.

Jesus says, the Kingdom is about the inward state of a man or a woman. It's about whether or not he or she is surrendered to God in Jesus Christ. It's about receiving what God freely offers as a gift, for the dying and rising of Christ. It's about offering everything you have and are and realizing what his love will do with it. It's about making the most important decision in your life.

'Lord, we feel that your word goes very deep into our lives. We sense the presence of Jesus, risen and Lord, and we know that we can hide nothing from him. So grant, Lord, to those of us who have never committed our lives to Christ, and who feel that you are calling us; grant us courage and grace to respond to your love with our love; to your giving of your life for us with the giving of our life to you. And to those who know you but have some things to get right, or some new dedication we need to make, or some new area of service for which to offer ourselves, or something which we need to get right with you; Lord, give us grace so to do. We thank you for the Gospel of the Kingdom. Lord, let us live in it to the full. Through Jesus Christ, our Lord, we pray. Amen.'

3

What Difference Does It Make?

Theorizing about Jesus and God is fine. Listening to people talking about how they've had insights into Christianity can be inspiring. But, actually, what difference does it make?

Billy Graham tells the story of travelling one night on a plane, where an extremely large man was drinking far too much and becoming very difficult to handle. Indeed, he got up and started walking up and down the aisle threatening people, with air hostesses following him up and down and one of the members of the crew trying to push him down. He was so large, they couldn't move him, and he just walked up and down, issuing threats left, right and centre. And then, suddenly, his eyes lit upon Billy Graham. He said, 'Is that Billy Graham?' And they said 'Yes, it is.' He staggered across the plane to Billy Graham and put out his hand and said, 'Dr Graham, I wanna tell you, you're preaching sure helped me!'

Well, we Christians, I think, are only too aware that maybe we don't look different enough. After all we don't dress differently and, by and large, we cannot immediately be recognized as different in our work, or in our home, or in the things we do. So what is the difference? What difference does it make?

Well, since we're asking about Jesus, I go back to some of our Lord's own words. Jesus said, 'Repent, and believe in the Gospel.'[1] I think if you work it out you'll see that the only real difference about the Christian is likely to be that he or she believes in Jesus. After all, other people meet for worship; other people have warm relationships with others who agree with them; other people give themselves in work outside; other people pray; other people reflect seriously about life; other people have thoughts about what happens after death. The only really distinguishing thing about us is that we believe in Jesus.

'Believe in the Gospel.' I want to point out six things about believing; if you like, six definitions of faith as Christians understand it, as they are given in the New Testament.

The first is this: faith is believing the truth of somebody or something. That is, you can say, 'I believe in somebody' and you mean 'I think he's got it right.' 'I think she's true. I think she's authentic.' 'I think he's got it all together.' You might say that in the situation of a strike union members will be saying, 'We believe in our union leadership.' No doubt in such a set of circumstances, many managers would say, 'We believe in our Managing Director.' The accent may be different but what is intended is the same; he's a man of integrity, he's a man who's got it right. That is the way in which Jesus invites us to believe. He said, 'Repent and believe in the Gospel.' But gospel – the word 'gospel' – originally did not describe something written down. We've come to use the word *euangelion* to mean 'something written down'. It meant originally a great, world-transforming event or, more properly, the news of a great, world-transforming event. The birth of Augustus was described as an *euangelion*, a 'gospel', a 'good news'. Jesus from the beginning makes it clear that the good news that we're asked to believe somehow centres on him. Indeed, Mark makes it abundantly plain because he calls it, 'the Good News of Jesus Christ' – 'the Gospel of Jesus Christ', 'the Good News about Jesus Christ'.[2] So when Jesus says, 'Believe the Gospel', he is saying, 'Believe in a world-shattering event.' Who or what is the world-shattering event? 'I am. I am.'

Therefore the disciples had, bit by bit, to wrestle with how they were going to respond to that. Bit by bit, it dawned on them that the distinctive thing about them was that they believed in him. That's why, as the story unfolds, certain descriptions are used of Jesus. That is, the emphasis is not on how they were tied to him in a personal, friendly way. The emphasis, again and again, is upon how they were tied to him in relation to ways in which he was described. 'Son of God', Peter says at Caesarea Philippi in a moment of great inspiration (which very quickly passed from him because he got into trouble almost the next breath!). In that moment of great inspiration he said, 'You are the Christ; the Son of the Living God.'[3] Jesus is recorded as describing himself often as 'Son of Man', which does not actually emphasize *only* humanity, it emphasizes something about God's *chosen* person. Sometimes it's 'Lord' (*Kurios*) – a word with a history also going right back into the Old Testament. Sometimes it's 'Saviour'; you remember the baby was to be called 'Jesus, for he shall save his people from their sins'.[4] Sometimes it's 'Emmanuel' ('God with us'). Sometimes it's 'Word of Creation'.

I emphasize this because I take it to be of fundamental importance in the New Testament. When we talk about believing in Jesus, there is a content to it. It's not believing that here was once a nice man who did good things, and who better for an example? That's very thin indeed in terms of New Testament interpretation. It's a person about whom they say: Son of Man, Lord, Saviour, Emmanuel, Word of Life. And every one of those ways of describing him is throbbing with meaning.

When I did my National Service – I was trained to be an education officer – there were forty-eight of us on the course, and forty of us were graduates. We had it on pretty good authority that they'd rarely had, as they said, 'such a shower' to train! We actually had one man who couldn't get straight the business of putting his left leg and his right arm forward at the same time. On one occasion, he actually lost his rifle. What was worse for him, he had an uncle who was an Air Commodore, which he was constantly reminded about. Part of the torture, which was called 'training', was that each of us had in turn to teach the rest a particular piece of drill, and we were examined for our 'officer qualities'. There was an airman who had about three thousand flying hours – a pilot of very great experience – and he was told to teach us how to 'right dress'. For the non-militaristic, I'd better explain that 'right dress' is a way of getting three rows of airmen straight. You tell them to fall in – in the technical jargon, 'get fell in' – the marker goes to his place, the three rows fall in on the marker. When the command 'Right dress!' is given, you take two steps forward, turn your head to the right, put your arm up on to the shoulder of the next chap, look along the row until you're focussing right along a straight line, and shuffle till you're straight. When you're straight, you hold it, with your eyes looking that way until the officer in charge says, 'Eyes front!' Well, our selected instructor explained that very carefully indeed. He told the marker to fall in, he told us to fall in, he shouted, 'Right dress!' We put up our arms, we looked along, we shuffled to and fro till the lines were straight. Then we realized that he'd forgotten one thing. He didn't tell the marker to stand still. The marker, being an arts graduate from Bristol University, could not resist the occasion! He waited until the three lines were all very straight, and then *he* started to shuffle! At this our instructor became absolutely speechless, as three rows of airmen wafted across the parade ground, like trees in a breeze, moving steadily out of sight! Only the officer in charge brought us back to order as chaos ensued.

All we needed was a marker. We knew everything else. We just wanted somebody standing still, on whom the rest of us could be focussed. That is exactly what the New Testament says about Jesus. Jesus is offered as God's marker. When they say, Son of God, Son of Man, Lord, Saviour, Emmanuel, Word of Life, it's all a way of describing God's marker for faith.

It is for this reason that it is important that we believe things about him as well as believing in him. If you can believe that he is the Son of God, then you are saying something not just about yourself, or even just about him; you are saying something about the universe; you're saying that it is personal. As the little girl said to her Mummy, 'Isn't it true that God is a bit like Jesus?' If you can call him 'Son of Man', then you're beginning to grasp something about God's plan in history: about Jesus somehow being representative of all of us. If you call him 'Lord', then you're beginning to understand that the Christian life has to do with obedience, with being 'under orders'. If you can call him 'Jesus', which means 'Saviour', then you're beginning to enter into the possibility that whoever you are and whatever you've been, forgiveness is available. And if you can call him 'Emmanuel', and understand that it means 'God with us', then you have a chance of walking out and saying, 'I saw God in things today I've never seen him in before!'

> Heaven above is fairer blue,
> Earth around is sweeter green.
> Something lives in every hue,
> Christless eyes have never seen

wrote the hymn writer, somewhat romantically.

> God of concrete, God of steel,
> God of piston and of wheel,

wrote Dick Jones, more prosaically and realistically. But, you see, you're saying that once I see God in Jesus, I begin to see him everywhere! If you can call him 'Word of Life', then the whole world is open to you.

But it all depends on being able actually to know the truth about Jesus.

People say sometimes, 'I'm a Christian because it makes my life so different.' 'I'm a Christian because I find the fellowship so helpful.' I have to say, 'I'm a Christian because I believe it's true!' And if it didn't make me happier, I hope I would still be a Christian, because it's *true*! And when life really destroys you, when people around fail you, when things go wrong, when it's one of those dark days, however you care to describe it, that's not reason for not being a Christian! The reason for being a Christian is Jesus is true!

So faith is not primarily a feeling. It's not whipping up some kind of enthusiasm which you see in others. Faith, first and foremost, may be about saying, 'What do I think about this Jesus? Do I think he's "Son of God"? Does "Son of Man" describe him? Is he "Saviour"? Does he strike me as "God with us?" Does he look like "Lord of Life"?' – and so on. Faith is accepting the authenticity of someone – Jesus Christ.

Secondly, faith is responding to what God has already done. For the words of Jesus from Mark 1.15 are more than simply 'Repent and believe.' He says, 'The Kingdom is at hand. Repent and believe.' That is, he is saying first that God has done something, and that to believe is to respond to what God has already done. That's why the Christian church makes so much of sacraments. There's nothing particularly special about water, or bread cut up into squares or shaped into wafers, or wine of varieties of kinds, that would make them the centre of some great festival. If, however, that water is about God gathering us into the experience of what he has done through Jesus Christ; and bread and wine represent for us the body and blood of Christ, then of course it has meaning. Therefore, when we baptize, in whatever way we baptize, or when we take bread and wine, whatever we call it, we're saying our way of believing is a response to what God has already done for us.

Therefore faith has to say 'What do I think God has done in Jesus?' That is, how much importance do I attach to the fact that God has already done something in history which has not only divided history into BC and AD, but actually changed the whole possibility of history? God has written himself into history for keeps. What would be the appropriate response to that?

Professor Mascall once wrote in most daring words, 'Christianity stands or falls by certain events alleged to have taken place in a remote part of the Roman Empire nearly two thousand years ago.' That's nice and sharp. He's saying God has acted – how do you respond? For the one thing you can't do about history is rub it out. You may wish it hadn't happened, you may try to change it, but it's there. And while it's there, you have to ask, 'What am I going to do about it?'

Well, the message is that God has said in Jesus, 'I love my world, and I love it altogether, and I give myself in love to it.' I ask you what the appropriate response might be. To have faith is to see that God's love is such that I want to give myself back to him who gave himself for me.

Thirdly, faith is an avenue of God's power. In another part of Mark's Gospel are those quite staggering words of Jesus when he says, 'If you have faith as a grain of mustard seed, you will say to this mountain, "Be removed hence!", and it will go.'[5] Now that was a particular way of trying to make a point, a point that Jesus is trying to make in a whole variety of places: that faith becomes an avenue of power. You can discover, if you like, that you are 'plugged in' to a new way of life. The people who came to Jesus and began to trust in him found that they could do things they didn't think they could do before. When Jesus gave them a kind of trial run as apostles and sent them out two by two, they came back and said, 'Master, it's wonderful! We actually cast out demons in your name! People come who are ill, and we heal them in your name!' And Jesus says, 'Yes, I saw Satan fall from heaven.'[6] Why was that? Not because he taught them some magical tricks, but because they'd been with him. They'd somehow got in on what he was about, and as a result what he did they could do.

The story of walking on the water is a difficult one. But what it's saying is that when Peter fixed his eyes on Jesus, even walking on water seemed possible. As soon as he looked away he went straight down. While he had his eyes on Jesus, it was possible! After the resurrection, in the Acts of the Apostles, you find them trying this out again. A man at a beautiful gate said 'Give me money'. Peter says, 'We haven't anything. But in the name of Jesus Christ of Nazareth' (he'd learnt that, you see, when Jesus was still there) 'in the name of Jesus Christ of Nazareth, rise and walk!'[7] The man leapt to his feet! Luke doesn't say who was most surprised, but he leapt to his feet. Peter had discovered again that when you are in on what Jesus is by faith, you can do what Jesus did. That's what Jesus said: 'In my name you'll do greater things than I've done.'[8] He was assuring them that faith can be a way in which power somehow comes to you.

I remember Leslie Davison, a previous General Secretary of the Methodist Home Mission Division, telling a story of a little charismatic prayer group he'd gone to in a private house. He said when it came to the prayer time somebody from the back of the room simply stood up – he heard the movement – and then said, 'Lord, you know me. I'm George. I used not to be able to put two words together in public. But it's not like that now, Lord! And I thank you.' And he sat down. Leslie Davison said, 'I felt as though I was in one of the earliest Methodist class meetings; that a bit of divine power had touched a man in a place where he thought there was no life. And suddenly he'd come to life.' To believe in Jesus is to establish by grace a link down which line all kinds of surprising things come. I guess that if Christians made more time to share with one another their own experiences, they would hear story after story to illustrate this point.

What you plug in to is the whole life of God revealed in Jesus. So sometimes it's judgment. After all, Jesus said to Peter, 'Get behind me, Satan!'[9] Sometimes to be plugged in to Jesus is to receive the power which condemns you for being wrong. Sometimes it's a call: he said, 'Follow me.' 'Take up your cross.' And sometimes he's saying, 'Why don't you move out? Why don't you try something more ambitious for me? Why don't you stop getting stuck?' Sometimes it's forgiveness – I sense mostly it's forgiveness. Mostly, it's Jesus saying to us, 'You are hard on yourselves. Why can't you believe that if I can accept you, you can surely accept yourself?' Sometimes it's a gift of healing. After all, he healed people. Sometimes it's encouraging; sometimes it's growing – he helps us to grow; sometimes it's learning to pray, learning to read the Bible, learning to enjoy worship; his gifts are endless!

I went to Korea and was introduced to a number of Korean meals. The first challenge to Europeans at a Korean meal is that before you get into the room you've got to take your shoes and stockings off and put on slippers because all floors are beautiful and polished. The second problem is that you've got to sit right down on the floor and the table is about one foot high so you've got to get your knees somehow under the table if you're going to get anywhere near the food. Once you're into that situation (which can be a very painful one!) the food starts to come. At my first experience of this they brought us in a few little bowls which had some soup and meat and vegetables. I thought it wasn't all that much for a special meal, but since we were eating it with chopsticks, I needed all the time I could get! But for the next hour they kept bringing more bowls – more meat, more fish, more vegetables. Then we moved on to the sweet – bowl after bowl. The table was absolutely packed with little bowls. We sat for an hour as delicacy after delicacy was provided. I thought it's a bit like being a Christian. You start off because something draws: maybe it's forgiveness, maybe it's service, maybe it's truth, maybe it's the fellowship. You start off with the one thing. You think maybe it's not enough for life, but it's enough to get on with. The life of the Christian is a life in which again and again

Jesus offers himself to us in all forms. If you go only after an experience I don't believe you ever get it, because what you experience comes out of your relationship with him. The search to be a Christian must always be a search for Jesus, not for an 'it'. It is as we give ourselves to him and relate to him and his power that we discover what experience he has for us.

The fourth thing is that faith is a way of perceiving truth. In one passage of the Bible there is a single statement including the very interesting words: 'By faith we know.'[10] In other words, faith helps you to see that things aren't actually always what they seem. After all, Jesus wasn't. He seemed like an illegitimate after-thought, born so far out of the way that you wouldn't have known about it. 'At the wrong time in the wrong place', you might say. When he started to teach, he told such simple stories that people listening might have thought 'Well, anybody could tell that story.' The disciples he gathered around him weren't outstanding. If he wanted to impress people, he could have chosen much better than that. Yet the thing about Jesus was that he was not what he seemed to be. When he started forgiving sins, healing people, telling the authorities where they were wrong – it wasn't what was expected of him. If he was going to be a Messiah, to get crucified was not the right thing to do. In some ways he was himself a living parable; and once you begin to be in Jesus you perceive that things aren't what they seem to be.

Before we were married my fiancée and I went to visit a theological college in Ireland. As we walked into the grounds, there was the man doing the garden. He wore wellingtons, an old woolly jumper and a battered old trilby, and he was pushing a barrow with a spade in it. We said we'd come to visit the college and that I was teaching in another theological college. He said, in a lovely Irish brogue, 'Well, would you like to see round the college?' I said, 'Yes, we'd like that very much.' He started to show us round, and I was telling him about theological colleges. As we proceeded it seemed to me he knew an awful lot about the life of the theological college for a gardener. It was only later we discovered he was actually the Principal, one of the best Old Testament scholars in Ireland at the time. We thought he was the gardener! He wasn't what he seemed to be.

I believe that, once you begin to trust in Jesus, you discover that life is like that. Life isn't about matter, it's about person. At the heart of the universe is not an 'it' or a power, but a 'he', a person. Which means that all offences against person are offences against God, but that everything that plugs into the personal is somehow related to God. It means that the power Jesus speaks of isn't superior human force. One of the most powerful persons in the world is a baby: a baby which cannot feed itself, cannot tell you what it wants, cannot get up and run away or come towards you, is absolutely helpless, and yet reorganizes the entire household.

Jesus kept trying to say that power isn't power as we understand it. 'The poor in spirit own the world', he said. 'It's the meek who've got it all under control. It's those who hunger and thirst for righteousness who are fulfilled.'[11] Now that's nonsense! – or it's profound. Satisfaction doesn't come by getting, but by giving. Suffering isn't the worst thing, hardness is. Some of the darkest days are some of the most beautiful if you're in Jesus. The more you go on with him, the more you begin to see his presence all over the place. That's what the parables were about.

> The station brook to my new eyes,
> Was bubbling out of paradise

as Masefield's converted villain says. Same quality of water, same name; just now its source is somewhere else.

Many years ago I was travelling on a train, and changed at Birmingham (as one usually does), and standing on the platform next to me there was a young couple. There were some cases. It was quite plain – they were in such distress – that one of them was going and the other was staying. When we got into the compartment, she got on and he stayed off, so he put her into the same compartment as myself. I didn't have to listen to hear the conversation – I couldn't help it. They had about ten minutes before the train was due to go out. They spent the entire ten minutes discussing whether or not he should go now, to lessen the pain of watching her go out, or whether he should stay and get every last second of her presence. The entire ten minutes was taken over by the discussion. I thought she must be going to

Alaska or somewhere! Then in the conversation – this was Tuesday – it transpired she was coming back on Friday! But they spent the entire time – from which you'll gather that she won and kept him there – they spent the entire ten minutes wrestling about this. I felt like saying, 'Excuse me, do you know anything about therapy? Have you heard anything about group relationships? About focussing on the brightest element in the situation? She'll be back on Friday.' And then I thought, 'No, I will listen to this.' Because it was love at a very deep level. It was love somehow bringing suffering upon itself in order to celebrate its loveliness. As the train pulled out and he stood there absolutely shaking – he was sobbing! – and she was standing there heaving at the window, I thought, 'I'm pretty near to God here. Something very deep is happening.' Peter Berger would call it 'a signal of transcendence'; or as Ian Ramsey put it more simply 'the penny dropped'.

To be in Jesus is to perceive things that you did not see before.

Faith, fifthly, is giving your life to somebody else. Jesus did not say, 'Believe in the cross'; he said 'carry it'. He did not say, 'Stay here and think about what I'm saying to you'; he said, 'Follow me.' Again and again, those men and those women who followed him were asked to commit themselves wholly to him, so that even when he died they did not escape. They now became the followers of the man for whom they had hoped many things, but who was indeed crucified. The women standing at the foot of the cross carried all the pain that was involved in being a follower of something that had gone wrong. He expected them all the time to give themselves to him. That's why baptism and our communion service are about death and resurrection. Believing in Jesus is not a matter only of the mind or of the emotion: it's also a matter of the will. It is saying to him, 'Lord, I die with you', to everything that is contrary to God's will, and 'I rise with you', to everything that is God's will. That is going to be the ruling principle from now on. I don't know of any more stirring challenge than that: to give my life wholly to him who died for me and to rise with him to everything that is God's will. Of course we don't achieve it – of course we don't! But that's the principle on which we operate.

When I was being trained in a theological college, I went to sermon class. Week after week I watched my fellows trying to conduct a service and to preach. Then we all went round to the classroom and criticized. My turn came. Then it was over, and somebody else's turn came. I found that, week by week, my understanding of what a sermon should be was steadily rising. My insight into what a good act of worship might be was steadily being raised. I've never achieved it – but I can never forget it either. That's the aim, now. Living with and for Christ is to have one's ideal of the good life steadily raised.

To belong to Jesus by faith is to say, 'Whatever of self stands in the way of God's will, I die to that, today and forever. Whatever in me can be opened to God's will, I want it to be open and always open, and more and more open.' Every day, it's to learn to say no to that selfishness which is opposed to God, and yes to that openness which is his will.

I once went to fly in an aeroplane with a man who is a friend of mine. We had to go to play a game of football and then, when we came back, he had some spare fuel. He said to me when we came back over our station, 'Are you feeling all right?' I said, 'Fine thank you.' He said, 'Right, I'll show you what this aeroplane can do.' It could do everything! It could fly upside-down; it could fly the right way up; it could go this way; it could go that way – very fast! It could swing to the right; it could swing to the left; it could do just about anything you wanted to do. He just kept on making it happen. I kept on saying to myself, 'He is a good pilot. He has lots of experience. He has never crashed before. The Meteor is a good aeroplane. The RAF have been using Meteors for many years. Very few ever crash. Engines do not fall out of aeroplanes. Neither do passengers!' It was the only way to survive, for I was entirely in his hands.

Now, I read not very long after that an article in the Officers' Christian Union magazine in which a pilot described his training to fly a plane. He reached the point when he had the instructor behind him, but it was his flight. The instructor said, 'When this one's over, you'll fly on your own.' He did everything well, according to the book, and then the instructor said, 'Let's see how you are on pulling out of a dive.' He knew what to do; he put the plane into a dive, and they started to go down to the ground.

Somehow, seeing the ground coming at him at such a speed just froze him. The instructor said, 'OK sonny, pull her out now.' But he was rigid. They were going nearer and nearer to the ground, and the instructor said a little louder, 'All right, son. Pull her out now', but he couldn't do anything. Then he heard the voice of the instructor, 'Son, just take your hands off the controls, will you?' He did so and slowly, the plane pulled up. The trainee wrote in his article, 'Only a few weeks later, it was as though I heard Jesus saying to me, "Son, why don't you take your hands off the controls of your life and let me fly it with you?"' It was his testimony. He'd lived it out first in flying terms, and then it had happened to him morally and spiritually. He was learning to commit his life.

The last thing is that faith is the springboard for action. Much that is written here might give the impression that Christianity is a very interior thing and it is. It's very much a matter of relationships with God at an individual level. Jesus turned crowds into groups of individuals when he started speaking about God. It is also about a faith which is lively, which is active. It's about a faith which reaches out and does things because it is now linked with Jesus. If you want to follow Jesus, then you'll have to discover what it is to be a person of the works and words of Jesus. Jesus healed, didn't he? How may the church be an agent of healing today? Jesus fought injustice, didn't he? How may we fight injustice in our world today? Jesus sought peace, didn't he? How may we reach out for peace in the area? So one could go on. At every point, what Jesus was is what we are called to be. So a faith which says, 'I'm happy now, thank you, I don't need to go outside the church, I just like the meetings here,' is not true faith. Dr Kenneth Greet a former President, and Secretary, of the Methodist Conference, once said to me, 'I find it hard to believe in the authenticity of a conversion which does not produce a profound change in one's social attitudes.' I think there's a lot of truth in that. Conversion to Jesus should bring a profound change in your social attitudes because now you see it as he sees it. Starving people are not just a tragedy, they're a blasphemy! For his heavenly Father gave enough food for everybody. People who are underprivileged because others are selfish are not just a problem. Their condition constitutes a blasphemy because they should not be so; we should not allow them to be so! Every problem in the world – the destroying of the world's resources, the problems of ecology, the problems of racism, the problems of people dominating others – they're all offences against the loving Creator.

To follow Jesus is to be a disciple, is to be one who commits himself or herself to *doing* something in the world. And Jesus says, 'If your faith doesn't do anything, I really doubt whether it's faith.' 'Show me your faith without your works', says a New Testament writer 'and I'll show you my faith by my works.'[12] When Jesus called, it was always a call to do something.

So, what is faith? Faith means believing something about Jesus. I don't mean that you need a theology degree before you can become a Christian. I mean there is a truth about him which is at the root of everything else. Faith means to respond to Jesus, because he is God's action in our direction. Faith is an avenue of God's power. It is to discover that things we did not have, we have; things we could not do, we can do. Faith is a way of perceiving that, beyond what is obvious in life, there is a whole hidden world of reality which he reveals to us by faith. Faith is a foundation for action, for doing things. And faith is giving your life into the hands of Jesus. It is what is different about us: faith in Jesus Christ.

I want to say to those of you who have never committed your lives to Christ, any one of these ways of faith is a way in. There are more, but there are, at least, six doors. Any one of these ways will establish a link with our Lord Jesus Christ. The rest will follow. To those of you who maybe think they're Christians but aren't sure, faith is a way of assurance. God has given his word to us, Christ has given his life for us, the Spirit is wishing to operate within us. Why not by faith respond to all of that? Those who are Christians may need to get something right. Well, it is by faith that we say, 'Lord, take it away! Put it right! Let me now be right with you!' Or maybe some simply feel they wish to rededicate their lives. Maybe it's got a bit tired; maybe it's got a bit lifeless; maybe it's time to say to the Lord again, 'I want us to be lively in our relationship, Lord. Let all this power and all this meaning and all this perception become real for me.'

'Father, in the many words, help us to discern your word. In the many words to many people, help us to hear your word to us, to me. And grant us, Lord, as once Jesus did in his physical life, grant us to know, as we hear his words, who we are and what our needs are. Help us to be able to believe things about him. Help us to be able to respond to what you have done through him. Help us to know the power of being linked to him. Help us to perceive the hidden things of life which can be seen in him. Help us to give ourselves in trust that we may be cared for by him. And help us that our faith may perceive what it is called to do, that in the world we may serve him. And if, Lord, you are calling us publicly to testify to our commitment or our recommitment or to our getting right with you or to whatever, grant us grace and courage not to turn away from your word, but to respond to your loving actions in Christ that we may be wholly yours. We ask our prayer through Jesus Christ, our Lord. Amen.'

4

Why Was He Killed?

I ask the question: 'Why was he killed?' It is a question that must be asked and answered. It doesn't make sense that a man to whom so many good deeds are ascribed should end up suffering a criminal's death. I ask it also because the Gospel writers are obviously so concerned with the death of Jesus. A third of Matthew's Gospel, a third of Mark's Gospel, a quarter of Luke's Gospel are taken up with the Passion of Jesus. We have to ask ourselves why men who undoubtedly were seeking to tell a story which would commend itself to many, spent so long on what seems to us to be an extremely gloomy topic?

Why was he killed? You can say, 'Well, he was one of those idealistic young rabbis who happened to get across the authorities.' The religious leaders didn't like the implication of some of the things he was saying theologically. The Romans by and large seemed to have thought he was not too bad in terms of his theology but were afraid of the public effect of the things he was saying, not least his references to kingship. The crowds were apparently easily manipulated one way or the other. The disciples sometimes grasped what he was about and sometimes didn't, and if they didn't they were pretty good at running away. You can, if you like, try to offer that as the answer to why Jesus was killed. It's a familiar story.

When I worked in Nigeria, however, at the theological college where I taught we used to have visiting speakers and one of them was a Nigerian magistrate. Such people can be very lonely in their work, and he spoke about the loneliness of having to preside in court, and how sometimes he wondered whether anybody was telling the truth. I fancy our own judges probably often feel the same. Afterwards I asked him how he decided on his response in such a lonely and puzzling setting. He answered, 'I find one criterion very helpful: does the story sound likely as it is being told?' That had a certain meaning for me because, just a few days before, I'd been in court and heard an old man explain that he had not actually been riding a motor cycle which had knocked somebody over. He said he'd been walking around an island pushing the motor cycle when a lorry came from behind and pushed it out of his hands, after which it then went right round the island and knocked somebody else over! I was in need of the criterion of likelihood.

Well, is it likely that Jesus would be put to death for the reasons I've offered so far? Is it enough to say that he was a good man who got on the wrong side of the authorities? For myself I have to say that I'm not gullible enough to believe that, and for the following reasons. First, right from early in the story Jesus is recorded as saying such gloomy things as, 'While the bridegroom is at the feast, people celebrate. When the bridegroom is taken away' – which is a curious word for going on honeymoon – 'when the bridegroom is taken away, then they fast.'[1] That sounds more ominous than a honeymoon to me. Then there is a question about the meaning of his baptism by John. Why was he baptized when baptism was for sin, and as far as we could see, there wasn't any? Or what about the temptations? Why did he have to face the temptations about ways of pleasing the crowds, and why did he resist them? Why did Jesus early in his ministry talk about the way the Jews treated the prophets – stoning them to death? Why was John the Baptist's death 'a sign concerning the Son of Man'? Why are the religious leaders shown as opposing him so very early in the story? Why did he go to Jerusalem when he knew they were determined to remove him? Why on the way to Jerusalem did he say, again and again, 'The Son of Man *must* go to Jerusalem, *must* suffer many things at the hands of the chief priests and scribes, and be put to death'?[2] Why does Luke describe the transfiguration in terms of Moses and Elijah talking to Jesus about his 'exodus'?[3] – that's the literal word. Remember how the Jews made their exodus, with the sacrificing of the lamb, and the putting of the blood on the lintel. Why did he not escape from the garden? What is the meaning of the prayer in Gethsemane? Why, when he was asked to defend himself, which he could have done so eloquently, did he not say anything? Why was he constantly using that little Greek word which we translate 'must'? Why 'must' he? Why did the Christians after his resurrection make so much of the death of Jesus as fulfilling the Old Testament prophecies, 'that the scriptures might be fulfilled'?

I think it is because the answer to the question which I offered earlier simply won't do. There is, beneath the surface of the events, much more than a young idealistic rabbi getting across the religious and secular leaders, having crowds who could not be predicted and disciples who could not be depended on. In Acts 2, Luke records Peter putting it quite plainly. 'This Jesus', he says, '. . . you crucified and killed by the hands of lawless men' – now that's precisely the earliest explanation I started with. 'This Jesus . . . you [Jews] crucified by the hands of lawless men' – that's the Romans. But I have actually given you only part of what Peter said. He actually said, 'This Jesus, delivered up according to the definite plan and foreknowledge of God, you crucified and killed by the hands of lawless men.'[4] In other words, Peter is saying that under the surface, through all the acts that were so varied and complex, as Jesus moved steadily towards the cross, God's will was being worked out. Somehow God was going to bring out of untoward events that which would be called 'gospel', 'good news'.

Now, if that's the case, what does the cross mean? Why was Jesus killed and why would God allow such a thing to happen and then use it for the good of the whole world?

I'm told that in Mozart's *Jupiter* symphony there are five main themes which, in the end, are brought together in fugue in thirty bars. Thirty bars of music bringing together fifteen themes. Now, you don't have to know that to enjoy the *Jupiter* symphony. You don't have to understand anatomy to use your body properly. If you really want to understand things however, it is worth going to that depth. And that's what we need to do in answering the question: Why was he killed? Why did he die? What does the cross mean?

On one occasion I visited Waterloo. There I went into one of the halls where the battle of Waterloo is presented in a series of murals. You stand on a platform in the centre and right round the wall are painted the murals. Marshal Ney is pictured riding into battle with his red hair flowing because he was caught out and rode into battle without his hat. There are horses and soldiers lying dying, all round. In order to grasp the battle of Waterloo through these murals, you ought really to be put on a swivel and to be moved so fast that you can see all the pictures at once. Since that isn't possible, you look at them one at a time and try to hold them together. That's what we've got to do if we want to understand the cross. We may not pick up Mozart's five-times-three themes in thirty bars, but sometimes it's helpful just to isolate each in turn.

Why did he die? It was a proof of God's love for us. Paul says in Romans, 'At the very time when we were still powerless, Christ died for the wicked. Even for a just man, one of us would hardly die, though perhaps for a good man one might actually brave death; but Christ died for us while we were yet sinners, and that is God's own proof of his love towards us.'[5] The death of Jesus is God's way of saying through his Son, 'I love you so much that even the cross is not too much as a way of demonstrating it.' That's why the cross is about God's love. It's about God saying to us, 'You really do matter to me that much.' It may be that this is one of the themes we need to hear more and more clearly.

There are so many people who do not believe that they matter; so many who do not believe that anybody cares. This message of the cross is one which comes to us as it came in a sense to the prodigal son before it actually happened, having claimed his inheritance and wasted it in a foreign country and now making his way home. The prodigal son was so concerned that when he met his father he'd have the right speech, and so he rehearsed it. It was a rather odd speech really. Fancy asking your father to take you back as a slave in the household. It was quite inappropriate to the occasion, because what mattered was not whether he had a nice speech ready to persuade his father; what mattered was whether his father loved him or not. He ought to have known his speech was not even necessary when, as he arrived – as we would say – at the end of a rather long drive, his father was standing, watching. He'd probably been away ages, but when he got there, there was his Dad looking down the drive! He should have known at that point that he didn't need any speech. But, like him, we also worry ourselves about: Do we understand it enough? Are we good enough? Have we done enough? Are we clever enough? Are we eloquent enough? Are we respectable enough? Are we whatever-it-is enough we think we should be? And God is simply saying, 'I love you. I love you. What more do you need?'

In the church in which I was minister in the north-east, there was a lovely little lady. She'd been retired many years. Her family were way away from her and, very sadly, first the sister with whom she lived died and then she herself became very seriously ill and we knew it was a terminal illness. She went into the hospital, and they said, 'Where are your nearest relatives?' When she told them, they raised their eyebrows a little: whatever were they going to do on all the visiting days? But she was absolutely inundated with visitors! When Christmas approached, every wall in her little room was plastered with Christmas cards, which the youth fellowship put up. She was a little lady who did not judge herself to be important at all. But God, through his people, plastered her wall with Christmas cards. Before she died, one of the nursing sisters said, 'Were you pulling our legs about not having any relatives? Where do all these people come from?' And she added, 'And what about all these parsons? Where do you get them from?' My friend said, 'They're all my special family.'

There are people who feel they don't count, who feel that it doesn't matter what happens to them. I heard at a theological conference many years ago now a lecture on what was called 'the black experience'. I thought it was going to be about the dark night of the soul, but it turned out to be the religious experience of black people in America. The lecture was given by a professor from an American University and his wife sat at the piano playing all through the lecture. It was fascinating; she just kept on strumming for an hour while her husband read poetry and gave his lecture. And, at one point, he read a little poem called 'Strut on, little sister' – you can imagine the music for that one, I'm sure! It was the story of a lady who spent her weeks scrubbing floors. She went into the offices when nobody was there, so no one ever spoke to her at work and all the time that she was in there she scrubbed floors. She really didn't count at all. But on Sunday morning she dressed in her best. There was only one 'best', as it were, and all the rest was a long way from it. On a Sunday morning, about thirty seconds before the service was due to start, so that the only seats vacant were at the front, and everybody was there, focussing on her, she walked down the aisle in her best. And the poem said, 'Strut on, little sister'. She had thirty seconds of glory once a week in the House of the Lord. Which things are a parable . . .

I believe that God says to us, again and again, 'Don't worry about whether you are good enough. Don't worry about whether you know everything you need to know. Don't be anxious if you can't get everything right doctrinally. Don't go on blaming yourselves if you don't get everything right morally. The ground of my loving you is that I love you. And the proof that you belong is the death of Jesus.'

Secondly, it was God's sacrifice for us. The death of Jesus is not just a demonstration of love: it has to do with sacrifice. The writer to the Hebrews says 'He', that is, Jesus 'has appeared once for all at the climax of history to abolish sin by the sacrifice of himself. And as it is the lot of men to die once and after death comes judgment, so Christ was offered once to bear the burden of men's sins.'[6] It is not only a demonstration of love: it is a sacrificial act.

Now, there's nothing new about sacrificial acts. Any of you who have been in Derbyshire may have been to the little village of Eyam. In the village of Eyam at the time of the plague it was discovered that the plague had got into the village and therefore the vicar called all the residents together and said, 'In the interests of everyone else in this area, I believe that we must contain the plague in the village.' Remarkably, they agreed. If you go to the village of Eyam today and walk around the village, you'll see outside so many of the cottages a little board. In each case, it has on it the names of those who died in the village of Eyam during the plague in order to contain it, including the vicar's own wife.

You could repeat story after story like that of sacrificial acts. Indeed, one of our scholars, F. W. Dillistone, has written a book demonstrating how this, again and again, happens in history; the sacrificial act that somehow is needed in order to stem some moral evil. The Jews who first came across these stories of Jesus of course understood what sacrifice was about. They'd been brought up on sacrifice. And although we don't find the Old Testament sacrificial system all that helpful it can communicate a great deal to us. It tells us something about God's nature as pure light. It tells us about how sin defiles the sinner. It says that sin is of life and death importance. It says that God, in his love, takes the initiative towards the sinner. It also says that the sinner does not simply stand back and watch it happen – he selects the animal to be offered. He takes the animal which is part of his own flock. He has to say certain words which identify him with the sacrifice. He has to wait to know whether or not he will be forgiven. The cross of Jesus Christ as sacrifice does not in any sense undermine God's love for us; rather it extends it, for it says the reality of sin in a moral universe is an extreme reality. It separates from a holy God. It defiles us. It defiles other people. It's a matter of life and death. And it requires that something be done about it. God offers a way whereby something may be done about sin, so that its sinfulness may be seen, and that it may be dealt with too.

I think that we need to hear that in other moods in which we find ourselves, for we are all prone (and there's a good deal of modern behavioural science to encourage us) to blame others for what we are. You know the story of the little boy who was standing, trembling, while his father read a ghastly school report that he'd just brought home? His father went down all the bad marks, reading one after another, his frowns deepening all the time. In the end, as a kind of gesture, the little boy said, 'Dad, what do you think my trouble is? Environment or heredity?' I'm told it didn't help a great deal.

Of course we are all influenced by what we have come from, by where and how we have been raised, by the society in which we now live, and none of us knows how much he or she is influenced by that. Of course that is true. It is equally true that one of the things which distinguishes us from every other part of the creation is our capacity to stand apart from ourselves and reflect on that; to try to work out and understand it as best we can, and then to seek to accept some responsibility for ourselves. As we accept some responsibility for ourselves, we – every one of us – would have to admit that we aren't even as good as we would like to be, let alone as good as God wishes us to be. And the cross is God's way of saying, 'You can't put it right. You can't get good enough to walk into my presence in your own right, for sin separates. But there is a sacrifice which I have offered in myself through my Son as a way of demonstrating sin's sinfulness and love's power.' And that's why, through the blood of Jesus, there is forgiveness. And that's why the Holy Communion means so much to Christians.

Miss Pauline Webb told a story of the time when she was visiting overseas, and she had a great women's rally at which to speak, with Holy Communion at the end of this great festival. She saw an old lady arrive, carrying her shoes, and thought it was a curious thing to see so she asked the story. They said, 'Well, she's come ten hours down the mountains.' When asked why she carried her shoes on this journey the old lady explained that 'you can scratch your shoes on the mountains'. When it came to Holy Communion and the minister said, 'Draw near with faith. Receive the body of our Lord Jesus Christ which was given for you and his blood which was shed for you, and feed on him in your heart by faith with thanksgiving,' the old lady slipped her shoes on, walked down the aisle like a queen, knelt at the rail to receive the bread and wine, the promise of God's forgiveness and cleansing and renewal. She then walked back to her seat, slipped her shoes off, and set off up to the mountains for ten hours. All the way down and all the way up, carrying your shoes lest you scratch them, in order to receive bread and wine which says:

Thy body, broken for my sake,
My bread from heaven shall be;

Thy testamental cup I take,
And thus remember Thee.

It is a sacrifice for us.

Thirdly, it is a ransom for us. It is a price that is paid on our behalf. The Old Testament and the Graeco-Roman world knew the use of the word 'ransom'. It was used in the Old Testament because they believed that the first fruit of everything should be offered to God. They had a sense that maybe the first fruit of the womb should be offered to God, but instead of offering their first child as a sacrifice, a ransom was paid. If someone was a slave and needed to be set free, a ransom was paid. If a man's ox gored another to death, then he was guilty of murder, but instead of his being put to death, a ransom was paid. A ransom is always the price paid to set you free from a guilt, a debt or a punishment. And this word is translated into the New Testament: 'You were redeemed [ransomed],' says Peter, 'not with perishable things such as silver and gold, but with the precious blood of Christ, as the lamb without spot and without blemish.'[7] Anselm in the eleventh century developed this theme in order to help people to understand that the whole point of this ransom was that God was taking the initiative to do for us what we cannot do for ourselves, because at the heart of our being estranged from God there is rebellion. Paul writes, 'For our sake, God made Jesus to be sin who knew no sin, so that in him we might become the righteousness of God.'[8]

I don't know about you, but there are times when I know that I have done wrong because I am rebelling. It is not just that I am overtaken by wrong; it is that I *choose* to do wrong. In those moments, I find it hard to believe that anybody could put me right. It is in those moments, therefore, that I need to hear that there is someone who has stood in for me to put things right for me. Even I as a rebel may hear the news that there is a way open, for Jesus has done what I as a rebel could not do. And since it sometimes sounds a little immoral that somebody else should do for me what I cannot do for myself, I would simply remind you that we are not left to face this reality as spectators. We are invited into what Jesus has done for us. He said, 'Carry your cross.' The message of Paul was, 'Be buried with him and raised with him.'[9] The cross does not invite us to stand apart and look and say, 'I'm grateful that I'm now forgiven.' The cross invites us ourselves to die and to rise with Christ. And that's a very much more meaningful thing.

If there are times when we need to hear simply that we're loved; and times when we simply need to hear that, although sin is a terrible and a spoiling thing, there is a sacrifice that has been offered for us; there are also times when, in our rebellion we need to hear that what we cannot do for ourselves to get right with God, Jesus has done on our behalf. 'There was no other good enough,' says the hymn writer, 'to pay the price of sin. He only could unlock the gates of heaven and let us in.' But it is not immoral, because I am invited to join in the death and resurrection of Jesus Christ every day of my life. That's no easy option.

The cross also means that God was fighting a decisive battle. Paul writes: 'On the cross he discarded the cosmic powers and authorities like a garment. He made a public spectacle of them and led them as captives in his triumphal procession.'[10] All through his ministry Jesus was fighting a battle against the powers of evil. All through his ministry he was seeking to show that sin need not have the victory.

Some of you who are not Methodists may not know it, but we have a Methodist minister who is an all-in wrestler. (You may feel you know many Methodist ministers who are all-in wrestlers, but I mean this one really is!) One day when we were travelling to a synod I asked him why he didn't play for our synod cricket team? 'Oh,' he said, 'cricket's much too dangerous a game for me!' So I took the opportunity to explain that it sometimes seems to me on the occasions I've watched wrestling on the television as though they fall before they're pushed. They seem to throw themselves across the ring before their opponent actually throws them. 'Is it all fixed?' I asked. He said that it was not like that at all. 'It's like this: if a man gets your arms in a grip and you go against the grip, he'll break your arm. If he has your leg in a grip and you go against it, he'll break your leg. So, when you're in a grip, you go with the grip. And, as you go with the grip, you try to think how you might get a better grip.' Well, I've never tried it, so I take his word for it.

As I reflected on that, I thought how profound it could be as a comment on our Lord's ministry. Why did he go to Jerusalem? Why did he wait in Gethsemane? Why did he allow them to take him? Why did he not defend himself? Why did he not call in just a little of that power that he seemed to have to do all kinds of marvellous things? Why did he never do that? The grip of evil was tightening on him all the time, yet he allowed it to happen. He went with the grip.

When finally they put him on the cross, it looked like the final, the eternal, half-nelson. As he hung there with his arms out, it was as though he was saying, 'Is there any other part of the grip you'd like to try? Is there any other way, any other thing, you'd like to do?' And when they took him down – to follow the metaphor, when he hit the canvas – they thought it was all over. But he was still going with the grip. He was taking all the force of evil into himself. When he rose on the third day, he was announcing that there is a stronger grip than evil, and that is love, and that divine love will always break the grip of evil in the long run.

I believe that's what the cross is about. It's about Jesus fighting on our behalf a battle which tells us that to describe sin as totally victorious is a 'con'. It is as likely that sin will ultimately triumph as that every girl using a particular kind of hair spray will get a film star husband, or that every man who gives Milk Tray by climbing mountains and flying through the air will get a beautiful girl, or that Heineken actually refreshes the parts which other beers don't reach. It's a 'con'. Sin is a 'con' in the world. And the word of Jesus through the contest was, 'You'll see the real end of the contest on resurrection day.'

There are times when I need to hear that. When the powers of evil in the world seem to be rampant or when, within my own life, I feel the pressures of temptation, then I don't need to hear simply that I'm loved, or that a sacrifice has been made, or that someone has done for me what I cannot do for myself. I need to hear a word which says evil will not in the end triumph. The only place I can see that is the death and resurrection of our Lord

Jesus Christ. I believe that it is the message for us to glory in today: that evil will not ultimately triumph.

The last thing is that the cross is God's invitation. The writer to the Hebrews says, 'Let us draw near with faith in full assurance, having our bodies washed with water and our minds cleansed'[11] – the invitation of the cross to join in the work of the Lord. If the message is that we are loved, then we are invited now to be channels of love to the poor, to the needy, to the underprivileged, to the hungry, to all who need us out there. We not only receive the love, we become channels of it. If the message is that a sacrifice has been made that we may be accepted by God, then we are called to sacrificial living ourselves. We are called to offer ourselves in his service in the world. If the message is that someone has done for us what we could not do for ourselves, then we are invited now to do for others what they cannot do for themselves. If the message is that a battle has been fought once and for all – our 'El Alamein' has been fought once for all on Calvary – and we enter into that, then the call is to fight that battle against all forms of evil. If the message is that there is an invitation to every one of us through the love of Jesus to live in the family of God, then we are called to take that invitation out to the highways and byways, wherever people may be.

The cross of Jesus is the most relevant fact, together with the resurrection, in the world today: for it is the only way we will find the life of God renewed amongst us and power for the church to do her work outside.

Let me finish with this. It may be that some readers have never actually come to terms with this. You've never seen that the cross is like this – you thought of it as something in history which was moving but not really relevant to your own personal life. It may be that you now see for the first time that the death of Christ is for you, and that it is for you the solution of your deepest needs. I would want you to have the chance to settle that matter with God. It may be that for some of you it is simply that your Christian life has become stale and that the story of Good Friday, the message of the cross, of God's love and sacrifice, his offer for you, his battle for you, his invitation, warms again that which was cold in your life. It may be you would wish to put that right. It may be that some feel it's right to make a rededication of themselves as Christians.

'Lord, we are sometimes surprised by what you say to us; always astonished at the depth of your will and mind for us. Grant us to be open to you, Lord. Where there are wounds which need healing, give us grace to come to you, the Physician. Where there is opposition which is built up against you, give us grace to come and bow before you in humility. Where we have chosen ways of life which have taken us away from you, grant us grace to choose again for that life which brings us closer to you. Where we have become lazy, grant us strength to be keen in your service again. Where our lives have lost their moral edge and things have entered in of which we're really ashamed in your presence, grant us grace to seek forgiveness and to find renewal and moral cleanness again. Where we have not properly grasped what it is about, help us to understand and to embrace the truth. Where we have slipped away help us to come back. Whatever our need, Lord, grant us grace to hear your loving word and to respond at the foot of the cross. We commend ourselves to you and pray for grace to do what we must do, through Jesus Christ, our Lord. Amen.'

5

How Could He Be Raised From Death

How could he be raised from death? I find myself somewhat criticized by my own text, for Paul writes, 'But you may ask how are the dead raised? A senseless question!'[1] The point which Paul is trying to make and which I want to take with absolute seriousness is that, of course, the question of how the dead are raised is not be any means the most important question. Even limiting ourselves to this one matter of resurrection, there is a variety of questions to be asked about the resurrection of Jesus Christ. Was it an historical event or not? If the Romans or the Jews took away the body, then why didn't they produce it when the disciples said he was raised? If the disciples took away the body, how did they prevent it from becoming a place of pilgrimage? How could they create a message which changed their lives morally if they knew it was a lie? If they made a mistake about the grave, wasn't it easy for someone to identify the right grave and to produce the information? It is sometimes said that Jesus didn't die properly at all. Well, just imagine what they did to him! Add to all that happened on the cross the experience of a cold tomb and a cold slab, and being totally covered in bandages as the bodies were. That kind of objection requires a greater degree of gullibility than the acceptance of the story as history.

Another possibility is that the resurrection story is a myth, in the best sense of the word (that is, it creates an artificial historical setting in order to communicate something which cannot be communicated except by creating a historical picture). I take that with great sympathy. I can understand why people like Bultmann and others have taught this – that is, Jesus did not physically rise from the dead, but that the truth of the Gospel is resurrection. I can understand why people come to believe that for the whole concept of a body being raised from the dead is so strange to us, particularly in a culture so dominated by scientific approaches to knowledge.

I have to say, however, that I do not myself find that acceptable, and for a number of reasons. One, I think that the way in which the writers tell the story, as opposed to the way in which they tell other parts of the story, gives the impression that they really do think they are recounting something that actually happened. The second reason is that the stories are divergent one from the other, which does not read to me like a group of people trying to create a consistent myth. It reads very much more to me like different people telling their view of something which did actually happen. Thirdly, I find it difficult to believe that there was no bodily resurrection simply because God in the Bible is constantly revealed as the God who acts in history and then interprets in a spiritual way. His people are brought out of exile and that means . . . The prophets proclaim a message and that means . . . Again and again, God acts and then interprets.

I have to say, therefore, that I find it most natural that God should raise Jesus Christ, his Son, bodily from the dead. Certainly, it is a likely way of illustrating and explaining the more important truth, which is that love will in the end triumph over evil and death. Certainly, the idea is more important. The New Testament writers are much more concerned about what it means than about whether they can prove it. This may be, in itself, an indication of their attitude to whether it happened or not. If they knew it happened why should they try to prove what they knew to be the case? Given its factuality, they move on to its meaning.

What then, does it mean? It means that God was saying something in the resurrection about Jesus Christ himself. Paul writes, 'He was declared,' – or the Greek word can mean 'designated' – 'declared [or designated] Son of God in power by his resurrection from the dead.'[2] The point is simply this: there were many teachers and healers in our Lord's day, many rabbis who gathered groups around them and who went out preaching and speaking. The question was: did Jesus differ from the rest and if he was different was he different in kind or different in degree? The resurrection of Jesus Christ declares that he was different in kind. He was not just more than all the other teachers or healers; he was different from them. The difference is primarily shown in that Jesus Christ was raised from the dead.

You know the story, I expect, of the French nobleman who went to a friend and said, 'I'm thinking of founding a new religion', to which the friend replied, 'That shouldn't be too difficult. Just get yourself killed and then rise from the dead.' It's a very serious point. Paul is claiming that God is saying through the resurrection that Jesus is different in kind from all other teachers, rabbis and prophets you have ever known or will ever know.

That is important because the fundamental question for us about Christianity is not 'Does it make you feel better?' or 'Do you join a nicer set of people?' or 'Does it give you a greater sense of purpose and peace?' or any of those other things which can be important. The fundamental question about Christianity is 'Is it true?' If it's not true, it doesn't matter how you feel about it. There were lots of people who felt better in following Adolph Hitler. There are lots of people who have felt better in following all kinds of prophetic leaders who seem to us to be members of the lunatic fringe. The question is not how you feel, or whether it suits you, or whether it settles into our culture nicely. The question is 'Is it true or is it not?' At the very heart of Easter day is the affirmation by God: 'It is true, because it is based on Jesus, and Jesus is the Son of God raised from the dead.'

To move, perhaps, away from the philosophical level to a rather more popular level, when Lady Diana became Princess Diana, all kinds of people asked, 'Will she be able to measure up to being a princess?' I think it is generally agreed – though I'm not a great reader of all the court circulars – that the tour of Australia answered the question. It was not that they gave her special injections on the way out to Australia, or that she had rehearsed certain parts. The question was 'Was she able for that task?' and the inter-relation of herself and her ability with the circumstances as they faced her demonstrated, in the judgment of many, that she was.

I believe that is what God is saying about Jesus Christ. He was born as a baby, he grew up as a child, he taught in very complex circumstances, he was put to death, and at every point there was about him that perfection of the Son of God which, nevertheless, had to respond and develop in relation to the situation. When finally God raised him from the dead, he was declared to be, designated to be, the Son of God with power. The resurrection is a statement about Jesus.

It is also a statement about what Jesus Christ came to do. You remember at the prophecy of the birth, as Matthew records it, the words read, 'You shall give him the name Jesus' – that is, 'Saviour' – 'for he shall save his people from their sins.'[3] But all of us know the sadness we feel on Good Friday. All of us sense the darkness that overtakes us then. We feel how untoward an event it was, how unacceptable, what a scandal that such a good man should be so put to death. The question which had to be asked, again and again, was, 'Was that the end of another lovely, idealistic, good man? Had the authorities won yet again by removing someone whom they resented as a threat?' As the story is told in the Gospels almost everyone involved seemed to have thought like that. The disciples fled; some women followers silently watched and wept; the religious authorities felt immense relief; the crowds had experienced another crucifixion, and the soldiers had simply done their job. The resurrection story flies in the face of every one of those attitudes. It says that Jesus had a purpose in giving his life for love of us and that what we came to do he had successfully done.

You remember those men who, in the fifteenth and sixteenth centuries, started saying silly things about the world being round when everybody knew it was flat? How much interest they aroused when they said, 'It isn't flat. You can't actually fall off the end. It does go right round and, what's more, it's possible to travel round.' Many people said, 'Hmm, interesting', but not many volunteered! The press-gangs got a good number of them to go. But some men said, 'It is round. And it is so round that it is possible to go round and come back and survive.' So they duly prepared; said their farewells which, as far as their relatives were concerned, were not *au revoir* but goodbye. They did not expect to see them again. Although the Monarch of the day sent them off with a fair amount of royal pleasure, I'm pretty sure they also closed the files. Nobody was waiting when they came back, by contrast with those who sail round the world today. There just was suddenly on the horizon a sail. Somebody with a bit of expertise said, 'That looks awfully like so-and-so's ship.' 'No,' they said, 'it can't be. He thought the world was round you know.' But, as the ship got nearer, it was him and his crew! And when they said, 'Where've you been?' they said, 'We've been right round. It is true! And we've demonstrated it.'

The death and resurrection of Jesus Christ say to us, as clearly as God can say in history, 'I love you, and I have gone all the way through death to demonstrate it. I have made the impossible round trip from life through death and back to life again. I offer you forgiveness, and the death and resurrection of Jesus Christ are the ground of the offer: a demonstration of forgiving love. I offer you the privilege of being the sons and daughters of God, and I have done everything I can to show you that you can trust what I offer.'

In the Old Testament, on the great Day of Atonement, there was a moment when the High Priest, having washed himself totally, wearing absolutely pristine garments, would go into the Holy of Holies. Only Jewish people were allowed in the court, and they would stand there, waiting. For one moment, this man, representing all the people, would go through into the holiest place where the Jews believed that the raw presence of God (if I may put it like that) was. Nobody went in except on these special occasions and, on this day, ceremonially, representatively, the High Priest went in. As he went through the curtain, everyone held his breath, waited to see whether divine holiness would destroy this fallible human being, or whether he would survive. Then, after a little while, out he would come – the curtain open, God's acceptance re-affirmed, and a great sigh of relief would go up. 'It's true! God still loves us and accepts us.'

The death of Jesus is so much more wonderfully that for us. How can we question God's love and forgiveness when he has gone through death and come back again to demonstrate it?

It is, thirdly, a demonstration that those who put their trust in him can have new life now. It was Bishop John Robinson who made the point during his lectures on Romans at Cambridge University that the dividing line in human experience is not a line drawn between life and death: it is a line drawn between being in Christ and out of Christ. That dividing line runs on through and beyond the grave. Therefore, the crucial dividing line is not something that lies ahead of us yet – 'When I die will I be all right?' The dividing line is now and runs out into eternity, and the crucial question must be, 'Am I in Christ, or out of Christ?' The resurrection is an invitation to join in life in Christ. Paul writes to the Romans, 'As Christ was raised from the dead in the splendour of the Father, so also we might set our feet upon the new path of life.'[4]

Christianity is not just about believing, it is about receiving. It is not just about getting some intellectual truth straight; it is about receiving into your life all that God has to offer. I remember many years ago going to Cliff College, the Methodist training college for evangelism in Derbyshire. It was in those days when for a young man to have very long hair was very new. For a young man to have very long hair and rather cool outfits was even more new. We had not seen much of it in those days. I went to Cliff College to address the students and they were, by and large, dressed extremely smartly – it was a very formal occasion. But when they stood up for a particular activity I saw standing quite near the back of the student body a tall blond young man whose hair was literally resting on his shoulders. He had a moustache and a beard; he looked as though he'd missed his way to Oberammergau. His outfit was very different from everybody else's, and I thought, 'I wonder who you are? I wonder how you got in? Do you belong here, or did you just slide in for the food?' He was introduced to me afterwards – indeed, he introduced himself, and explained that six months before he was living on the beaches of our country. He was going from place to place and he named the places where at that time it was popular for groups of hippies, as they were called, to be. He was part of that whole scene. Looking at him, I could believe it. He explained how a Cliff College mission came to the place where he was living on the beach so he decided to listen sitting on the beach – to these young men. He said, 'That changed my life. And I'm here now because those students came to where I was on the beach.' He's now a pastor of a free church. I quoted him because sometimes a striking illustration of something helps us to believe in the possibility of it in a less striking way. In other words, I don't believe that Jesus offers power only to men like that or women like that because I've seen too many ordinary men and women like you and me whose lives have been slowly changed by the power of the Gospel.

I spent part of one Holy Week in the garden. I thought it was a good thing between Good Friday and Easter day to plant some seeds. It seemed to be a symbolic thing to do. Now what I don't know about gardening is worth knowing! I'm entirely dependent on what the instructions on the packets of seeds tell me to do. But my credulity on this occasion was stretched to its limit when I opened one packet and poured some seeds on to my hand. They were so small that it was very difficult to distinguish them one from the other. With my large hands I did not find it easy to pick *a* godetia seed out and be sure it was there. When I started popping them in I could hardly see whether they were going in or not. Yet every one of those seeds (the packet says), every one of those seeds is full of life. Now where did it get its life from? Well, of course, it comes from a plant. Well, where did the plant get its life from? Well, it came once as a seed. Well, where did that come from? . . . and so on. And that's why Jesus said, 'I am the true vine and you are the branches.'[5] That is, when by faith we put our trust in Christ all the life of God becomes available to us. We may look to the world like little godetia seeds wrapped up in our little, white, hermetically sealed bags that we call churches. But actually, in Christ, we can be bursting with life. Easter day is the day which says so! Those who put their trust in Christ can know new life.

The last thing it does is to demonstrate the reality of life beyond the grave. Have you ever puzzled about the resurrection body of Jesus? I have. You see, as the story is told, it could go through walls and doors evidently and yet it could be touched. It needed to eat. Now, what an odd thing! What an odd thing to put into the story if you were trying to commend it unless there is some truth that is hidden there. I think the truth is actually plain to see. The writer to the Hebrews says, 'Jesus is the pioneer of our faith.'[6] That is he's always going from step to step ahead of us. The resurrection body is a way of assuring us that Jesus's resurrection is the first fruit of the harvest to which we belong. His progress through death, resurrection and ascension is a pattern for ours.

Sometimes, when I was teaching in theological college, students would say, 'I have a bit of difficulty with preparing a sermon.' I would say, 'Well let's have a little exercise together.' The student, or group of students, would come to my study and I would say to them, 'Choose a text.' When they had done so we would begin the process of preparing a sermon. We'd reach for commentaries; we'd ask about the historical background; we'd look for the setting of the text in the particular part of the Bible where it was found. Then we'd seek the main element in the meaning. Next we'd ask ourselves which points we wished to make in this particular sermon. We'd look for the applications of these main points. We would turn then to the question of illustrations. We'd follow that with work on how to start and how to end. After about two or three hours we hadn't got a sermon ready but at least we could see where we were going. Sometimes a student would say, 'You know, that has been really most helpful to me, just to start with a text and to see how you get to the point when you're in the pulpit.' Now that, to me, was proper teaching. It was going through the process, step by step, alongside a student in a way which helped that student to see that it was possible to get from the starting point to the destination, unlikely though it had seemed at the beginning.

In the same way, the resurrection body of Jesus is saying to us that our resurrection being will be related to who we are now, and yet not wholly limited to what we are now. It is a kind of recognizable 'I' or 'you', and yet it is recognizable in a different way. 'I in my resurrection body,' Jesus is saying, 'will give you an idea what it's like in transition.' That's why when in the garden Mary, thinking he was the gardener then realizing that he was Jesus took hold of him, Jesus said, 'Mary, do not keep on holding me because I am not yet ascended to my Father.' In other words, 'Mary, if you keep on holding me here, I'll never complete what I set out to do. There are other things to do yet. This is not the time to be standing hugging in the garden.' Mary just saw him and thought, 'How lovely! He's still here! What's the best thing to do? Hold him!' 'No,' he said, 'I've got to go on.' The resurrection body of Jesus is a kind of demonstration to us that it is possible to move from this 'I' to that 'I'.

Paul puts it rather differently. He says (to use our language), 'When you plant a bulb at sowing time, come the harvest if a bulb popped up through the ground and lay there, would you be pleased? Of course you wouldn't! You plant a bulb to get a flower. Supposing you put in a daffodil and what came up was a weed, would you be pleased with that? Supposing you put in a daffodil and got a tulip? Of course not,' says Paul, 'You put in a daffodil bulb, so you'll get a daffodil. Just as the bulb is fitted for life underground, so the daffodil is fitted for life above the ground. Try putting a bulb on the surface and see whether the flower grows under the ground. Silly!' says Paul. Exactly. 'Nonsense!' – he uses the word – 'Nonsense!' If you put a bulb in, you'll get a flower. If you sow a body in faith, you will get a spiritual body in glory.[7] And the body of Jesus Christ is God's way of saying, 'Don't worry.' It's like the young actor going into the great actor's studio and seeing him sitting there in open-necked shirt and jeans, and then watching the process whereby the actor becomes Coriolanus. Bit by bit, as each new thing is done, the young actor begins to see how this person is being translated into some other person for the play. The resurrection body of Jesus says to us this is how it is going to be. And one day, you'll have a spiritual body, totally fitted to spiritual reality and yet still fundamentally 'you'.

The last thing is by way of testimony – not my own but somebody else's. Russell Hindmarsh was a Vice-President of the Methodist Conference. He was a brilliant young physicist: professor of atomic physics at Newcastle University. He died of cancer in his early forties. We were good friends and when it was known that he was dying I travelled to see him and spent a day with him which I will never forget. In the course of the day we had some quiet conversation. I said, 'Russell, you may have things you want to say to me as a friend and, if you have, I wish you'd say them.' He said some things to me that I hope I will never forget. Then I said, 'Are there any things you want to say to me as a preacher?' He said, 'Yes. I have as a preacher studied for many years I Corinthians 15 about the resurrection from the dead. I have known it with my mind to be true – I've studied the commentaries, I've worked it out.' He said, 'Every day since they told me I was dying I have read I Corinthians 15 and I not only know intellectually something about it, I believe it with all my heart. It's true! We are going to be raised in Jesus Christ.' Now, he was not given to flowery language. He was not given to being excessive spiritually, but he'd come to that deep conviction that in Christ there is life beyond the grave for us all. And, since he gave me permission to say it, I say it.

Easter day is a glad day because it says something about who Jesus is: the Son of God with power. It's a glad day because it says that what he came to do – to die for our sins – has been done successfully. It's a glad day because it says that if we join ourselves by faith to him we can have the new life that comes to branches from the vine, to seeds from the plant. It's a glad day because it says that when we die we need not be afraid; we shall go to be with him forever in an eternity for which we shall be entirely fitted, just as we are now fitted for this. No sorrowing, no sighing, no more pain, no more separation, a life of love in Christ. Why should we worry about the detail of how it was done when the meaning of it is so eternally powerful?

'Grant, Lord, that the meaning of the resurrection of Jesus may dawn upon us today. Thank you that the resurrection makes clear that he was 'the Son of God with power'. Thank you that it demonstrates the indestructability of your love, even for us. Thank you that we can be joined by faith to what Jesus did for us in dying and rising. Thank you that his resurrection power is available to us today, to enable us to be increasingly like him.

Help us, daily dying with him to all that is selfish and evil in the world, daily to rise with him in experiencing resurrection life – a life committed to all that is good and lovely and true. We ask our prayer through Jesus Christ, our risen Lord. Amen.'

6

How Can He Be Known?

The question 'How can he be known?' is in some ways the most difficult of the questions we have faced so far. Let me start by making some qualifications about knowing Jesus. The first is that our language is very limited. When you are trying to describe something like a knowledge of Jesus Christ, Son of God, Son of Man, Lord, Saviour, Emmanuel, God with us, Word of Life, what language can you use? So I am comforted that we sometimes communicate in rather odd language. We say, for example, 'The kettle is boiling!' but we don't actually mean the kettle is boiling. If the kettle is boiling you really are in trouble! We say, 'It's raining cats and dogs', but we don't ring for the R.S.P.C.A. Each summer many of our population listen to the voices of cricket commentators telling us about a man with a short leg, a long leg, a square leg and a fine leg, and this strange beast actually sometimes bowls 'no balls'! But those who understand cricket as they hear the description can picture it exactly, because the language used is appropriate to the topic.

There are limitations to our knowledge too. It's not only our inability to describe it, it's our inability to experience it. I suppose that isn't surprising if we are talking about God himself. Whenever you talk about God, by definition you're talking about that which merges into mystery. If your knowledge of God is free of all mystery, I beg to wonder whether you actually know God at all. We may get some help by starting from another area of knowledge which is mysterious and profound – our knowledge of one another. Just as we can find language which serves as signal language, so we can look at our own experience of one another and say, 'How many people do I know or understand completely?' Answer, 'Nil, including myself.' Yet I can establish reasonable relationships with a large number of people whom I don't know altogether. I know enough to work on. I know enough to establish a relationship. Maybe if, in the limited mystery of human beings, we find it possible not to know everything but to know enough to establish a relationship, that should be a help to us in connection with our knowledge of God too. When dealing with that which is even more mysterious – the knowledge of God – we will never understand all. But can we not know enough to establish a relationship?

Maybe the third qualification should be that our modern age is often very impatient with us Christians. There has been a stage in the study of philosophy when we have been told that our language is nonsense, that we cannot demonstrate the meaning of what we say. I suggest that it is not that our modern age is so clever that it has seen the shallowness of what we believe, but that our modern age is so committed to instant solutions that it is too impatient to perceive the profundity of what we believe. The Prime Minister is expected to give answers to a television interviewer about the entire economy in about forty-five seconds. People have to expound serious topics on the media between cartoons, advertisements and entertainment. Technology provides us with the opportunities to make quicker and quicker responses. I wonder whether we haven't become an age which is so determined to have an instant answer for everything that we've lost the patience for the profound. Therefore maybe the incapacity of many of our fellows to perceive the truth of Christianity is not a sign of our weakness, but of the cultural atmosphere which we breathe every day.

Even with such qualifications, however, we still have to answer the question, 'How can he be known?'

He can be known wherever the Holy Spirit is at work. One of the greatest difficulties for the early disciples was that they were trying to handle something that they had never known before. They had been raised as Jews to say, 'The Lord our God, the Lord is *one*, and thou shalt love the Lord thy God with all thy heart, soul, mind and strength.'[1] 'The Lord our God is one' –

monotheism was one of the great distinctive marks of the Jews. Then, bit by bit, they found themselves thinking about Jesus in such a way that they got dangerously near, and then actually got to the point of saying, 'Son of God', 'Christ of God'; hearing him say things which put him on the other side of the line, if you like. Gradually they had to make room in their monotheistic way for God the Father and God the Son. Then just as their minds are beginning to grapple with this strange new feature of a God made man, however inchoate it was, just as they were beginning to grasp it, Jesus said, 'I'm going away.' Naturally they're very upset. 'Going away, Master? Where are you going?' Jesus's reply was, 'Don't worry, I'll send another.' You can almost hear them saying, 'Not another! Two is difficult enough: but three!' He used a word which means 'another of the same sort'.[2] Now they've got to handle God the Father, God the Son and God the Holy Spirit. Their understanding is neither clear nor profound but they are moving in a certain direction.

Jesus says certain things about this Spirit. He says, 'When the Spirit comes, he will teach you everything and will call to mind things that I have told you.'[3] That is, when the Spirit is at work, it isn't just a case of bringing a sort of feeling, 'I felt very emotional'. The Spirit testifies to content: 'He will bring to mind the things I told you.' The Spirit's influence is about knowledge, it is about content, it is about things to be believed. Jesus also said, 'He will confute the world [convict the world] and show where right and wrong and judgment lie.'[4] In other words, the work of the Holy Spirit is to draw attention to Jesus, not only in terms of the things he taught – that which is to be believed – but also in terms of the moral implications of what Jesus said and did and was.

Therefore when we think about the Holy Spirit, we should not think about a kind of a vague aura which produces a sort of emotion. The Spirit is much more precise than that. He brings to mind the truth, and he works out of us and with us and in us the moral implications of the truth. Jesus says, 'He will glorify me, for everything he makes known to you he will draw from what is mine.'[5] 'He will glorify me' – the Spirit isn't just about a feeling or about a content or about a moral implication, he's about glorifying Jesus. The Spirit's work is to bring commitment. So Jesus can be known wherever the Holy Spirit is at work, for he makes known the teaching, he makes known the moral implication of the teaching, he calls us out to commitment.

For Christians this is meant to be a regular experience. But there are also very special moments or periods of unusual insight, perception, revelation. Sometimes we discover things that have to be put right – the moral implications. At other times we are overwhelmed by a sense of what it means to worship Jesus in a new, in a deeper way. That's because the Spirit is at work.

I think John Wesley's greatest teaching was not about assurance, or about perfect love, but about prevenient grace. I don't mean he invented it, but he took this idea of 'grace which goes before' to mean that whenever we are challenged with a choice between good and evil the Spirit of God is at work making the choice for good possible. Whenever the Gospel is preached and men and women listen, the Spirit is at work already, making it possible to accept Jesus. If therefore we accept Jesus and are saved, we have nothing to boast about. We could not have done it but for the work of the Spirit. If we reject Jesus and are lost, we have nothing to complain about, for the Spirit was there helping us to believe.

Jesus may be known wherever the Spirit is at work and where the Spirit is at work people will discover truth to be received, moral implications to be acted out, and a challenge to be committed to Christ. Here is one answer to our opening question.

Jesus may also be known where the scriptures are read with understanding. The scriptures, after all, give to us the basic story. When I was a minister in circuit, we had a stewardship visitation, and one of the ladies came across one of those uncomfortable cases you sometimes meet when you're visiting; not a person who closed the door, or a person who was shallow, but a person who asked some very difficult questions. After a while, the lady visitor said, 'I'm sorry, you've got me beaten. I think you'd better see our minister.' So this lady was brought to me for a solemn interview. At the end of it I said, 'Look, if you wanted to learn German, you'd probably go to evening classes. If you wanted to learn music, you'd get a teacher. I teach Christianity twice a day on Sundays. I welcome you to church.' She came for about a month and then stopped. Months later, for reasons which I still don't understand, she appeared at a fellowship meeting – a Bible study. She walked home with a young student (one of the girls who was a member of our church) and this young girl was so perplexed by this lady who was asking such awkward questions that she just gave her testimony – that was all she knew to do. So she told how she had become a Christian. Early next morning, this woman rang me up and said, 'I want to tell you what happened last night. That young girl talked about her knowledge of Jesus. I went home. I felt absolutely depressed. I felt myself not to be a good person. I really felt oppressed by it all. I lay awake until suddenly, past midnight, it was as though the load was lifted from me. I went straight off to sleep, and when I woke this morning I still feel free! Am I all right?' I went round to her home and recited the words 'Come unto me, all ye that labour and are heavy laden, and I will give you rest. Take my yoke upon you and learn of me, for my yoke is easy and my burden is light, and you shall find rest to your soul.'[6] Her face just lit up! She said, 'That's it!' I said, 'Jesus said that.' Martin Luther called the scripture 'The cradle for the Christ child'. The story of God's great love for his people, the story of God's choice of Messiah, the story of Jesus fulfilling so much that was in the Old Testament: there it all is, set out in scripture. J. B. Phillips said that as he translated the New Testament he was aware of the presence of him about whom it spoke. When 'Metropolitan Anthony' was in his teens he read Mark's Gospel and became aware, as he read, of the presence of the one about whom it was written. The opening reading of the Bible led to the experience of the one who stands at its heart. This kind of testimony could be given by countless Christians.

He can be known where the sacraments are faithfully administered. When at Holy Communion we focus attention on the bread and wine, we are celebrating a number of things. We are celebrating our faith; it is an act of faith to take bread and wine and think of something else. We constitute ourselves the family as we gather round the table. We celebrate something about what God has done in Jesus, for it is his dying and rising which give meaning to the symbols of bread and wine. We also say something about bread and wine. We say that in this world in which we live material objects are capable, in the hands of God and in response to the faith of the people, of representing something entirely different. We are saying that the world is not, in fact, a material world only – that isn't the true story. We are saying that material objects can represent for us something very much deeper.

Canon Charles Raven – Professor Charles Raven – as a young curate in Liverpool during the time of the Depression in the thirties, was making his way home from a service at Liverpool Cathedral. In an area where there was a great deal of hunger and need and unemployment, he passed a fish and chip shop. By contrast with everything round about, the fish and chip shop was full of life and warmth and food and homeliness. People were crowding in, waiting with their money to buy their food and, as Canon Charles Raven put it, 'Suddenly the glory!' He suddenly felt, in the midst of all that dryness, God does care. There is food. God does provide. And a kind of vision came to him of a God of goodness and of love.

I suppose many of us have known this in the events of our lives. Maybe in the birth of a child; maybe in the presence of two people who love one another; maybe at the death bed of someone who is leaving us. Maybe in a moment when we have seen a beautiful sunset, heard a profound piece of music, read a lovely poem, seen a lovely act, watched someone gracefully moving about the world. It can be a thousand and one experiences or places! Suddenly we say, 'I wish I could keep this minute for ever!' For it points beyond itself to something else. Jesus can be known in the ordinary, everyday things as we begin to perceive their possibility. And that is why, as we break bread and drink wine, we shall be able to say, 'Jesus can be known as the sacraments are faithfully administered.'

He can be known where Christians live out their faith. Studies done in the United States reveal that eighty per cent of people who join the church do so because of the influence of a member of their family or a neighbour or a friend. That's hard for us preachers to bear, but it's the truth. Likewise eighty per cent of those who leave the church do so because they feel that the other members don't care whether they come or not. For many of us Jesus is known through people who love us and care for us.

I think of a Welshman called Ted Evans who worked at the iron company near to my home, and who took Sunday School week by week. He told homely, wise, Welsh stories in a mellow Welsh accent. I think of a man called Tom Dunn who took us when we were about fifteen years of age; who started every lesson all sweetness and light; who ended every lesson telling us that he'd put us out because we were so obstreperous and unhelpful. It was my punishment that, after he had died, his family decided to leave his hymn book and Bible in the pew, and it was the pew in front of the one that my family sat in. Every Sunday I went to worship, written on the top of the book were the words 'Thomas Dunn'. And every time I looked at it, I remembered what a bad time I'd given him in Sunday School. The times he threatened to throw us out! The times he told us we were lost to the Kingdom! But he always came back. Every Sunday he was there again. One of the things I must do in heaven is get right with Thomas Dunn. I think of Bill Stoddart, who was a giant of a man – huge – with a very broad Geordie accent. He used to stand in the pulpit and shout out, 'I thought I was a big man, till I met a bigger one!' He was a wonderful Christian witness: he would go halfway across Durham county if he heard someone had died, and would wait until the mourners had gone just to have a word with the nearest of the bereaved, to tell about the love of Jesus. I think about my Uncle Bill, whom I visited as he was dying. I was a young minister and I wanted to be there to minister to my Uncle Bill, who'd meant a great deal to me. He was almost dead, he could hardly put words together. I said to him, 'Uncle Bill, would you like me to pray with you?' He just nodded his head and said, 'Aye, I would.' So I knelt at his bed and I prayed. At the end of the prayer, there was a pause before I got up, and Uncle Bill started to pray for me! He was dead in ten hours, but the last sentences I heard him put together were prayers for my ministry.

I could use much more space on the people who have pointed

me to Jesus Christ. Hardly any of them were preachers – they were godly men and women in whom I saw Jesus Christ. We should not be too proud to want what they have got, and to seek to find it as they did.

He can be known in places of need. It was the shepherds who got the message about his birth – that's no coincidence. Shepherds couldn't get to the temple or the synagogue very easily. It's not easy to say to sheep, 'Don't go away, I'll be back in an hour-and-a-half. I'm just going to church.' So they were a bit 'out-churched'. How shocking that shepherds should get the message! There was something very significant about that. The place of his birth put him right alongside what we now call in the ugly modern phrase the 'marginalized'. When he started his ministry, one of the most shocking things was the way he mixed with the wrong sort of person. If he wanted to be a religious leader, of course he should have known better than that. Again and again, it was amongst the poor, it was amongst the needy, it was amongst the outcasts that he could be found, and it is so today.

Maybe if you want to see Christ at work you should go to Brixton, or Hackney, or Lambeth, or Poplar, and ask to meet some of the Christians there. Christians who, every day of their lives, are being treated wrongly because their faces are the wrong colour. Christians who, almost every day of their lives, are reminded that some people don't seem to think they belong here, though they were born here. They lack political muscle; proper education appropriate to themselves; proper housing; job opportunities; they are pushed down to the bottom of the pile, however you shake it; and they retain a marvellous Christian faith. If you want to see lively worship, go to Brixton and see how they worship God. Because life is immediate! The presence of God is immediate! Again and again, it is out of his people in need that God speaks his word through Jesus.

He can be known in the midst of life – ordinary, everyday life. I believe this is something which we Christians have not said enough about. Jesus can be known when men and women try to take seriously what it means to live an ordinary life. What it means to be a good father or mother. What it means to be a good husband or wife; a good employer or a good employee. What it means to handle one's gifts with care and reasonableness. What it means to be serious about our money and our possessions. I believe that it is as people are helped to ask the most serious questions about these topics that Jesus can be known.

One of the significant things about our church membership statistics is that more and more of the new members are young married couples with small children. It is not only because the Sunday School handles the children nicely. It is because the parents are suddenly facing responsibility for other lives, and they are beginning to ask, 'Have we got the moral quality to cope with these little lives that have now been put absolutely into our care?' I believe that it is as we begin to ask these very serious questions about what it means to be an ordinary human being that Jesus can become known.

He can be known in the life of the church. It is we who are in the church who sometimes find this hardest to believe. He can actually be known through us. I want to draw attention here simply to the act of worship. As I have already mentioned, I once went to Waterloo and into the rather expensive museum. When I asked where the actual battlefield itself was, they pointed me over to a few very innocent-looking fields, as they seemed to me. Then someone pointed out to me that there was a tower, up which you could go by climbing some 196 steps. We climbed up and up, I remember, and then we got on to the parapet. Then the Battle of Waterloo became almost totally intelligible. You could see the spot where Napoleon spent most of the day riding up and down on his white horse, right at the back of his horses. That's why Napoleon survived that particular battle. You could see the undulating of the fields, and understand why the French were so taken by surprise when, seeing the English army's retreat, they thought they'd won the battle, so charged forward. To their great dismay, when they came over the brow of a hill, there were the English squares, all waiting for them. Because of their position on the ground they weren't expecting it. They couldn't see it. But from up there on the tower it was abundantly plain that if only they'd had a helicopter and an intercom it need never have happened!

Now, I think worship is meant to be like that. In worship we need to say, 'Yes, I must not leave the world behind. My God is a God who's out there as well. But from here I see it differently. From here I see God in his glory, because I stop to think about him here. From here I see that qualities really matter most in life. From here I see that it is love and goodness and holiness and truth, that it is caring and reaching out and giving and helping, that really matter. It is here that I see that the slights I receive are nothing by contrast with what our Lord himself went through. It is here that I see that, with all the rush of life, it is a comparatively small span against the vision of eternity. It is here that I see that my problems are as nothing compared with the power of God. Here I climb the steps of the parapet and look out on the battle of life and it looks so different. And it is here that Jesus can be known.'

The sum of all this is that Jesus is willing to make himself known anywhere. If we are seeking to know him, he reveals himself. Of course we need the story as it is given through the church and in scripture; of course we do. Of course sacrament will help us greatly; of course it will. But at heart, it is a loving Father reaching out to loved creatures, reaching out to make us sons and daughters, and saying, 'If you'll just look this way, you will find in Jesus all that you need.'

Maybe for some readers this will be the first time to see it like this. Maybe you are able to say for the first time, 'Father, I give myself to you in Jesus. Thank you for reaching me here.' It may be that some of us are saying, 'Lord, I've been playing at this. It's much too deep for playing about. I give myself at the deepest level I know.' Maybe some of us are saying, 'Lord, I'm going to have to be different if this is true. I offer myself with the pledge of a changed life.' It may be that we have to say about our brother Christians, 'I give myself to them. I accept them. For they too are part of the family.' Whatever it is and wherever it is, God through Jesus reaches out in love and says, 'My hands are open. My arms are ready. My gifts are available. My love is never- ending.' Why hesitate to cast yourself right into the sea of his love?

'O God, even though I will never understand you wholly in this life, I am grateful that you show yourself through your Holy Spirit, in the Bible, through the Sacraments, in the witness of your people, at moments of need, as we explore the meaning of life and within the worship of your church. Help me increasingly to perceive your presence, to respond to what I perceive and to be committed to your purpose in my life and in the world at large. Amen.'

REFERENCES

Chapter 1 How Shall We Describe Him?

1. Mark 4.41.
2. Matthew 21.10.
3. Luke 5.21.
4. Luke 7.49.
5. Luke 9.9.
6. Luke 19.3.
7. Jean Paul Sartre, *Nausea*, Penguin 1965.
8. Anthony Harvey, *God Incarnate: Story and Belief*, SPCK 1981, p. 44.
9. Peter Hinchcliff, ibid, p. 88.
10. C. F. D. Moule in a New Testament lecture.
11. John Knox, *The Death of Christ*, Collins 1958, p. 70.
12. Mark 6.34.
13. Mark 10.14.
14. Luke 18.41.
15. John 11.35.
16. Matthew 21.18–19.
17. Mark 11.15–19.
18. Luke 4.1–13.
19. Luke 9.51–6.
20. Mark 14.32–6.
21. Mark 14.60–1.
22. John 1.27.
23. John 3.2.
24. John 4.29.
25. John 5.15.
26. John 9.24–5.
27. John 11.21, 32.
28. Mark 10.2.
29. Mark 2.18.
30. Mark 2.16.
31. Luke 11.39.
32. Luke 16.14.
33. Matthew 12.24.
34. Mark 15.31–2.
35. Matthew 16.16.
36. John 20.28.
37. Acts 22.10.
38. Matthew 5.17–48.
39. Mark 2.10.
40. John 3.18.
41. Matthew 7.22–3.
42. Luke 9.62.
43. Luke 14.26.
44. John 10.30.
45. John 14.6.
46. John 14.9–10.
47. John 8.46.
48. John 3.36.
49. Galatians 2.20.

Chapter 2 What Did He Teach?

1. Luke 11.20.
2. Luke 17.20.
3. G. Bornkamm, *Jesus of Nazareth*, Hodder & Stoughton 1973.

4. J. Jeremias, *The Parables of Jesus*, SCM Press 1972, p. 159.
5. Mark 2.22.
6. Matthew 20.1–16.
7. Luke 15.11–32.
8. Luke 14.25–7.
9. Luke 12.13–21.

Chapter 3 What Difference Does It Make?

1. Mark 1.15.
2. Mark 1.1.
3. Matthew 16.16.
4. Matthew 1.21.
5. Mark 11.22–3.
6. Luke 10.18.
7. Acts 3.1–10.
8. John 14.12.
9. Mark 8.33.
10. Hebrews 11.3.
11. Matthew 5.3–5.
12. James 2.18.

Chapter 4 Why Was He Killed?

1. Mark 2.19–20.
2. Mark 8.31.
3. Luke 9.31.
4. Acts 2.23.
5. Romans 5.8.
6. Hebrews 9.27–8.
7. I Peter 1.18–19.
8. II Corinthians 5.21.
9. Romans 6.4.
10. Colossians 2.15.
11. Hebrews 10.22.

Chapter 5 How Could He Be Raised From Death?

1. I Corinthians 15.35–6.
2. Romans 1.4.
3. Matthew 1.21.
4. Romans 6.4.
5. John 15.5.
6. Hebrews 12.2.
7. I Corinthians 15.35–49.

Chapter 6 How Can He Be Known?

1. Deuteronomy 6.4–5.
2. John 14.16.
3. John 14.26.
4. John 16.8.
5. John 16.14–15.
6. Matthew 11.28–9.